LITTLE LESSONS FROM THE FAIRWAY:
Spiritual Insights From the Game We Love

By Phil Ayres

Copyright © 2025 by Phil Ayres

All rights reserved. No part of this book may be reproduced or used in any manner whatsoever without the express written permission of the author except for brief quotations used in reviews or critical articles.

Printed in the United States of America

Greens & Grace Publishing (greensandgrace.com)
150 Sunset Dr
Longwood, FL 32750

This book is a work of non-fiction. Any references to real people, events, or locations are used for illustrative purposes and are not intended to defame or misrepresent any individual or entity.

Cover design by Joel Swan (@joelswan)
Cover photo by Jennifer Pedley (@picture1000wordsmedia)
Captured in 2009 on Hole #6 at Pilgrim's Run Golf Club

ISBN: 9798314612828

Praise for Little Lessons From The Fairway

"*Little Lessons from the Fairway* is an incredible devotional that uses the game of golf as a powerful metaphor for our walk with Christ. Phil Ayres, a trusted friend, pastor, and integral part of the *Keys for Kids* Ministries team, brings his genuine passion for both people and golf to every page. Phil's insights remind us that just as a proper grip can make or break a shot on the fairway, having God's grip on us is essential for a steady, faithful journey in life. Truly, this book is a must-read for anyone seeking a fresh perspective on faith and a love for the game."

—Greg Yoder, President, Keys for Kids Ministries

"James 2:26 says, '*For as the body without the spirit is dead, so faith without works is dead also.*' As a believer and professional golfer it's important to implement my beliefs in everything. This scripture helps me to go the extra mile while training if I truly believe in this gift I was given. Phil's book helps to integrate core scriptures into every day practice as a golfer. It's provides that extra push we need to keep getting better because believing in your ability is what makes anyone great in their craft."

—Daniel Augustus, Professional Golfer

"I've always felt closest to God on the golf course. As a friend—and now through *Little Lessons from the Fairway*—Phil has helped me see how golf, life, and faith continue to teach us, if we're willing to listen. He masterfully connects the discipline and humility of the game to deeper truths about character, purpose, and grace. As someone who works with golfers every day through

my clinic, *Full Swing*, I believe this book will resonate with anyone who loves the game and is open to life's bigger lessons."
—Dr. Chris Miller, Golf Physical Therapist
Full Swing Golf, Longwood, Florida

This book is a great resource for any golfer looking for small reminders and simple ways to reframe the mental side of the game. So much of it aligns with what I teach my golfers as a mental performance coach—not only about golf, but also about life. Phil has done an amazing job of creating something every golfer can relate to, with insights they can take away from any page they turn to."
—Chelsea Brooks, M.S.
Mental Performance Coaching

To my best golfing partner and the love of my life,
Stefanie—every fairway is better with you by my side.

TABLE OF CONTENTS

Acknowledgments 1

Foreword 3

Introduction 8

Playing Boldly 12

Art of The Swing 27

Practice Makes Progress 44

Honesty Is The Best Policy 54

The Scoring Game 64

Life on The Fairway 73

Trouble Shots 88

The Game Within 97

The 19th Hole 112

Pre-Round Devotionals 126

Acknowledgments

WRITING THIS BOOK has been a uniquely fun experience, much like a round of golf with good friends. I couldn't have done it without the support of so many people who have shaped my journey in both golf and faith.

First, to my kids, AJ and Sofie, and my son-in-law, Jack—your support and encouragement mean the world to me. Thank you for always believing in me, whether on the course or in life.

To my closest pals, Ken, Chip and Mark—our rounds together have been filled with laughter, competition, and the kind of friendship that makes golf more than just a game. I wouldn't trade those moments for anything.

A huge thanks to Joel Swan for his incredible cover design and to Matt Clark for helping with the pesky interior layout. Your talents made this book not only readable but also beautiful.

Thank you to Jennifer Pedley for being able to find the amazing photo that she shot back in 2009 at Pilgrim's Run. By far, my favorite golf photo of all time on my favorite golf hole!

To my LifePoint Church family—thank you for being such a great place to grow, serve, and share life together. And to the students at Freedom Christian Academy, your love and respect remind me why teaching is such a gift.

A special thank you to Dr. Chris Miller and the team at Full Swing in Longwood, Florida, as well as Wills Murray, Chelsea Brooks, Paul Henderson. Your guidance has helped me get closer to that elusive 10-handicap—I'm still chasing it!

To my Monday night Top Golf league crew—thanks for the fun, the competition, and the support. Golf is always better with good people around you, and I'm grateful for each of you.

Finally, to every golfer who has ever stared down a tough shot, fought through a slump, or walked 18 holes searching for something more—this book is for you.

Foreword

I HAVE BEEN FORTUNATE enough to witness the magic of professional golf in some of the most prestigious settings in the world. Attending major tournaments such as The Open at St. Andrews and The Masters at Augusta National feels like walking on hallowed ground. The history, tradition, and excellence that these venues represent are palpable, and the atmosphere is nothing short of electric. What makes these experiences even more remarkable is the dedication of the people behind these iconic events and courses who take their role as stewards of these sacred spaces seriously. They ensure that each blade of grass, each piece of the course, and every aspect of the tournament reflects the care and respect that the game of golf demands.

I serve as the CEO of Christian Financial Resources, where we have the opportunity to partner with hundreds of churches across the United States on stewardship. One of the closest partnerships to our ministry office is with LifePoint Christian Church, which has always held a special place in my heart. I was there on the very first day it was launched, decades ago, and over the years, I have watched as Phil Ayres and his team have built a thriving, impactful congregation that touches lives and spreads the love of Jesus in profound ways. Phil stewards his responsibility like he is taking care of one of those iconic golf courses.

Phil is not only a friend but also a deep thinker, a tremendous encourager, and an exceptionally effective pastor. He has a unique way of blending his love for the church with his love for the game of golf. Over the years, I have had the privilege of spending time with him on the golf course, where we've shared everything from strategic discussions about the game to meaningful conversations about life, faith, and leadership. What stands out the most to me is how his ability to grow both as a pastor and as a golfer reflects his character: humble, dedicated, and always striving to be better.

When Phil told me that he had written this book, I was genuinely excited. I knew it would be an incredible exploration of his two greatest passions—his faith and his hobby. The intersection of these two areas is a powerful one, and this book reflects the wisdom and insights Phil has gleaned from both his personal walk with God and his love of the game. It's a rare gift to be able to draw connections between one's faith and something as seemingly mundane as a sport, but Phil does so effortlessly in a way that makes you reflect on both the deep truths of the gospel and the simple, everyday moments that often go unnoticed.

One of the greatest blessings in life is finding a hobby that not only provides joy but also serves as a gateway to deeper personal reflection and spiritual growth. Golf, like many other hobbies, has the power to transport us from the challenges and stresses of daily life. A round of golf can be a brief escape, a way to reconnect with God's creation and experience the beauty of the world around us. It's also a unique opportunity to form meaningful connections with others. Golf is often played in pairs or small groups, and there's something special about the camaraderie that develops on the course. The conversations, shared laughter, and mutual encouragement are just as much a part of the game as the skill and strategy involved. It's a microcosm of life, where patience, perseverance, and the ability to enjoy the journey are all tested and refined.

Of course, golf can also be incredibly frustrating. The game has a way of humbling you—whether it's a missed putt, a poor shot, or simply the unpredictability of the elements. But despite the challenges, there's no place I would rather be. Whether you're celebrating the thrill of a perfect drive or the satisfaction of sinking a long putt, golf has a way of lifting your spirits and changing your perspective in an instant. And those moments—the ones where everything clicks, and you feel a sense of accomplishment—stay with you long after the round is over.

I've had the privilege of witnessing two of my playing partners hit hole-in-ones—a feat that remains elusive to Phil and me (we're still waiting!). There is an indescribable joy that comes from sharing in those once-in-a-lifetime moments. But what is equally precious are the deep, thoughtful conversations that have unfolded during our rounds together. Conversations that I carry with me long after the golf course is behind us, as they have shaped my thinking, deepened my faith, and strengthened my resolve. Some of my best memories have been created during golf trips with friends, where the shared experience of the game becomes the backdrop for lifelong bonds and unforgettable stories.

Phil has always had the heart of a teacher. He is constantly looking for ways to communicate life's profound truths through simple visuals and relatable stories. This book is a perfect example of that. Just as Jesus used parables to illustrate deep spiritual lessons, Phil uses golf as a way to reveal God's truth. It's a beautiful fusion of faith and sport, where the wisdom gleaned from the course can help navigate the challenges of life. I pray that as you read these pages, you too will be inspired to reflect on the lessons that golf—and life—have to offer.

Imagine, if you will, a beautiful day on a stunning golf course you've never played before. Phil is your playing partner. As you stand on the tee, preparing for your first shot, know that you're not just about to embark on a game of golf, but on a journey of reflection, growth, and inspiration. Phil's words will guide you, offering not just practical golf tips, but godly wisdom that will resonate long after the game is over. *Enjoy your round!*

Darren Key
Chief Executive Officer
Christian Financial Resources, Inc.

Introduction

GOLF HAS BEEN A LIFESAVER FOR ME. I didn't grow up playing the game, and I haven't been at it as long as many, but when I finally picked up a club, I wasn't just looking for a sport—I was looking for relief.

At the time, I had been a pastor for about five years, and the weight of ministry was catching up to me. The church where I serve (I'm still there, by the way) is a small-to-medium-sized congregation, but in those early years, I felt like a one-man band. I answered phones, managed the website, coordinated the worship team, led Bible studies, and, of course, poured myself into writing sermons each week.

I was running hard but running empty. That's when my wife, wise as ever, suggested I take up a hobby—something that would force me to take a real day off. Golf seemed like a good idea. I had played only one time before that, in an event called, "The Pastor's Masters," a local four-person scramble for ministry leaders. I was terrible. My pastor friends had a good laugh at my expense, playfully reminding me to "stick to preaching."

So, with a borrowed set of clubs and a pair of golf shoes I found at Goodwill, I headed to the course. It was a Monday, nice and quiet. Nine holes later (and about 60 strokes in), I found myself in the clubhouse, making small talk with a gentleman who turned out to be the club owner. When he found out I was a pastor and also knew a thing or two about websites, his ears perked up. He needed someone to redesign the club's site so golfers could book tee times online. His proposal? If I helped him out, I could golf as much as I wanted—free of charge. That was an easy yes.

A few weeks later, I figured if I was going to keep playing, I should at least try to get better. I booked a lesson with the club pro, thinking I could afford one or two since I wasn't paying for tee times. After our first session, he said, "Hey, I hear you're building the club's website. If you could do the same for me, I'd be happy to teach you for free. And your family too." I just about fell over.

I took it as a sign from God. Really. Here I was, trying to honor the idea of Sabbath, intentionally stepping away from work to recharge, and here He was, handing me this incredible blessing—free golf, free lessons, and a newfound love for the game.

I became *obsessed*.

And let me tell you, golf has a way of getting into your bones. It latches on and doesn't let go. Now, believe me—

I'm no pro. My game hovers around an 11 handicap, which means I can usually navigate the course in the mid 80s, but I still find myself making doubles and the occasional triple bogey. While my own game is always a work in progress, I've had the privilege of helping other golfers—mostly beginners—take their first steps or continue their journey in this great sport. Just this year, I have the opportunity to lead the golf program at our local Christian educational facility, *Freedom Christian Academy*. Guiding the next generation into the game and watching them discover all it has to offer is one of the great joys of my life.

Golf is more than just a game—it's a teacher. It reveals your character, tests your patience, and humbles you like nothing else. It connects you to people and, if you let it, to yourself. And yes, I believe it can even connect you to God.

This little book isn't just about golf tips or how to knock a few strokes off your game. It's about the lessons golf teaches—the ones that shape you, challenge you, and sometimes, even surprise you. My hope is that these simple reflections help you not just play better, but live better. Play the game for more than a score. Play it because, in so many ways, it reveals the real you. Thanks for reading, see you on the fairway.

PHIL AYRES
March 4, 2025

CHAPTER I

Playing Boldly

"Take dead aim."

- Harvey Penick

Play Your Game

When I was new to golf, I asked my coach how I could spin the ball backward on the green. I had seen the pros do it—hitting their approach past the pin and then pulling it back like it was on a string. It looked like magic.

He looked at me and asked, *"Do you usually hit the ball past the pin?"*

I thought for a second and said, *"No."*

He smiled and said, *"Then why would you want it to spin backwards?"*

That was the day I learned an important lesson—not just about golf, but about life. It's tempting to want what other people have. Maybe it's someone else's perfect swing, their ability to chip and putt, or even that shiny new driver in their bag. But the best players don't waste time wishing for another golfer's skills. They focus on improving *their own game*.

The Apostle Paul understood this, too. When he wrote to his friends in Philippi, he said, *"I have learned what it is to be in need, and I have learned what it is to have plenty. I can do all things through Christ who strengthens me."* (Philippians 4:12-13)

Contentment isn't about having the best of everything. Contentment is about making the most of what *you* have.

So don't worry about spinning the ball back if you're still

trying to hit the green. Don't chase someone else's game—just play *your* game and learn to love it as you improve.

⛳

Just One Ball Needed

I'VE NEVER QUITE UNDERSTOOD why some amateur golfers step up to the first tee with two balls—one on the tee and another tucked in their pocket. That second ball is there *just in case* the first shot goes bad. But to me, carrying that extra ball is a quiet admission of doubt. It's like telling yourself before you even swing, *I'm probably going to mess this up.*

Instead, why not step onto the tee with confidence? Trust your preparation, your swing, and your ability to put a good strike on the ball. If, for some reason, you don't hit it quite the way you'd hoped and your buddies grant you a "breakfast ball," then calmly walk back to your bag, grab another ball, and try again. But don't stand over that first shot expecting failure.

How often do we step into situations with doubt already in our pockets? We prepare for failure instead of expecting success. But Scripture tells us to approach life with a different mindset. *"Do not throw away your confidence; it will be richly rewarded."* (Hebrews 10:35)

Confidence doesn't mean perfection. It simply means trusting in what you've been given—the skills, the preparation, and the grace to try again if needed. So next time you step onto the first tee, leave that second ball in your bag and trust the swing you've got.

⛳

ARNOLD PALMER'S PRAYER

THERE'S AN OLD JOKE ABOUT A GOLFER playing at Arnold Palmer's famous Bay Hill course. When he reached the 18th hole—a forced carry over water of about 150 yards—his caddy told him, "Right here is where Arnie said a little prayer, pulled out a six-iron, and stuck it to two feet."

Inspired, the golfer bowed his head, whispered a prayer, and pulled out his own six-iron. He swung… and topped the ball straight into the water. Frustrated, he looked at his caddy and asked, "What did I do wrong?"

The caddy shrugged. "Not much. Only difference is—

when Arnie hit his shot, he kept his head down."

Prayer is a lot like that. Some folks think of it as a magic formula, like rubbing a genie's lamp. Say the right words, and God will grant your wish. But real prayer isn't about getting what we want—it's about aligning our hearts with what God wants.

The Bible tells us, *"If we ask anything according to His will, He hears us"* (1 John 5:14). Sometimes that means a "yes," sometimes a "no," and sometimes a "not yet." But the confidence we gain through prayer isn't in always getting the answer we hoped for—it's in knowing that God's will is perfect.

Just like Arnie could flush an iron shot under pressure, prayer gives us the confidence to move forward, trusting that God's got our best interests at heart. The key? Keep your head down. Trust the process. And know that whatever the outcome, you're in His hands.

A Mark That Matters

WHILE IT'S NOT AN OFFICIAL RULE, the *Rules of Golf* strongly recommend that every player mark their ball before the round begins. It's a simple step, but an important one. There are plenty of stray Titleists, TaylorMades, and Callaways scattered along the rough and beyond the fairway. The last thing you want is to play the wrong ball and take a penalty when a little ink could have saved you the trouble.

For me, I put a small plus sign on either side of the logo. That way, if I'm searching in the weeds or the woods, I don't have to guess—I know it's mine. Some people put a single dot, others use their initials. Some even draw a lucky symbol. It's a personal touch, but it serves a purpose: identification.

I wonder if that's the same idea Paul had in mind when he told the Ephesians that believers are *"marked with a seal"* by the Holy Spirit (Ephesians 1:13). Just as we mark our golf balls to prove they belong to us, God marks His own—giving us the Holy Spirit as proof that we belong to Him.

In golf, that little mark prevents confusion, keeps us from unnecessary penalties, and reassures us when our ball is found. In life, the mark of the Holy Spirit does the same—it sets us apart, guides us, and reminds us of whose we are.

So before your next round, take a moment to mark your ball. And as you do, remember—you've been marked, too. And that's a seal that won't fade.

Dollar-sized Divots

One of the first things my coach taught me about ball striking was to pay attention to my divots. He used to say, *"A good shot leaves a good divot."*

He wasn't talking about taking big chunks out of the course. He meant that a divot tells a story. A *dollar-sized divot* means you hit the ball cleanly, compressed it just right, and took a shallow, controlled cut of turf. A deep divot? That means you hit it fat. No divot at all? You might have caught it thin.

And direction matters too. A divot pointing left or right can reveal a swing path that's off. If you want to know how you're striking the ball, just look at what you leave behind.

Reminds me of life in general. Every day, with every word and action, you leave a mark on the people around you. The question is—what kind of mark are you leaving?

A careless word, a thoughtless action, an impatient response—those can leave scars, deep and damaging, like a fat shot that digs up half the fairway. But a kind word, a moment of encouragement, a steady presence—those leave the kind of divots you *want* to see.

Jesus told His disciples, *"Let your light shine before others, that they may see your good deeds and glorify your Father in heaven."* (Matthew 5:16)

On the course and in life, the mark you leave behind

matters. Make sure it's a good one.

⛳

PLAY GOLF, NOT GOLF SWING

ONE OF THE WORST HABITS I PICKED UP early on was trying to make my swing look perfect. I'd stand over the ball thinking about every little movement—where my hands were, how my hips turned, whether my backswing was just right. I wasn't playing golf; I was stuck playing "golf swing."

My coach saw what was happening. After a few too many overanalyzed shots, he pulled me aside and said, "You're thinking too much. Stop playing golf swing and start playing golf."

He was right. The point of the game isn't to have a perfect swing—it's to get the ball in the hole in as few strokes as possible. A beautiful swing means nothing if you don't score well. The range is where you work on technique. The course is where you trust what you have and play.

Life works the same way. It's easy to get caught up in how things look. We want to be polished, put together, and in control. But at some point, you have to stop overthinking and just do what God has called you to do. Ecclesiastes 9:10 says, "*Whatever your hand finds to do, do it with all your might."* That means being present, giving your best, and not worrying about appearances.

So when you're on the course, play golf—not golf swing. Set your target, trust your swing, and let it go. The best shots—and the best moments in life—come when you stop thinking so much and just play.

⛳

Measuring What Matters

Golf simulator technology is here to stay, and I'm all for it. I even run a weekly golf league at our local Top Golf facility. It's a great way to play the game, have fun, and sharpen your skills, rain or shine.

But I've noticed something over time—new players tend to get distracted by the wrong things. They get caught up in the numbers. Club-head speed, ball speed, launch angle—it's all there in bright, flashing digits. And sure, it's nice to know you can generate 165 mph ball speed, but if that ball is flying into the trees, those stats don't mean much, do they? In the end, the only number that really matters is your score. Whether it's a par, a bogey, or worse, the real goal is to keep the ball in play and get it in the hole.

The same principle applies to life. It's easy to obsess over numbers—credit scores, bank balances, social media followers, or even our golf handicap. But if those numbers don't lead to a richer faith, deeper relationships, or a more meaningful life, what's the point?

In Matthew 6:33, Jesus said, *"But seek first the kingdom of God and His righteousness, and all these things will be added to you."* He knew the importance of keeping the main thing the main thing. When our eyes and attention are fixed on what truly matters, everything else falls into place.

There's nothing wrong with keeping an eye on the details, just like a golfer should be aware of their swing tendencies. But don't let them become the focus. Let them be a gauge, not the goal. Because in golf—and in life—the numbers aren't what define success. It's about staying on course, finishing well, and making every shot count.

Your Swing, Your Calling

Having golfed these last 15 years, I've noticed that no two swings are exactly alike. Some are smooth and rhythmic, like Fred Couples. Others are unconventional, like Jim Furyk, looping and rerouting before striking the ball pure. Some swings look effortless; others look like hard work. But if they're repeatable, if they put the ball where it needs to go, then they work.

A good golf coach won't try to fit every player into the same mold. He'll take what a player has and refine it—strengthen the fundamentals, smooth out the kinks, and build a swing that suits that golfer's natural abilities. The worst thing a player can do is spend all his time trying to swing like someone else.

God didn't make you a carbon copy of anyone else. *"For we are God's handiwork, created in Christ Jesus to do good works, which God prepared in advance for us to do" (Ephesians 2:10).* That means He designed you with a purpose—your own gifts, your own story, your own way of making an impact.

Too many people spend their lives comparing their gifts to someone else's. But just like in golf, success isn't about imitation—it's about trusting how you were made. The key isn't to swing like someone else. The key is to let the Master shape you into the best version of who He created you to be.

So next time you step onto the tee and feel tempted to compare, remember: God made you different on purpose. And in the hands of the right Teacher, your unique swing—your unique life—can be used for something great.

Do You Have GAS?

THERE'S AN EPIDEMIC that has been plaguing the golf community for at least two decades. It's called *G.A.S. – Gear Acquisition Syndrome.*

Golfers with G.A.S. believe that a new driver will suddenly add 30 yards to their tee shots. They think buying the same putter as Scottie Scheffler will instantly shave strokes off their game. They watch golf club commercials like they're scientific breakthroughs instead of marketing campaigns.

Now, don't get me wrong—technology has improved. But the reality is, a bad swing with a brand-new club is still a bad swing. A slice doesn't care if you hit it with a $600 driver or one from a garage sale.

Over the years, I've given many new golfers the same advice I give people when it comes to buying cars: don't buy the newest model—buy one that's a couple of years old. The technology is still solid, but the price has dropped because someone else already broke it in. Same performance, less pain in the wallet.

And here's the most important thing—golf isn't won or lost with a brand name. The best equipment in the world won't save you if you don't learn how to move the ball around the course wisely and confidently. If you really want to improve and you have some money to invest in your game, you'd be far better off spending it on lessons rather than the latest driver. A good teacher can help fix flaws in your swing that no club ever will.

Proverbs 4:7 says, *"The beginning of wisdom is this: Get wisdom. Though it cost all you have, get understanding."* If golfers spent half as much time acquiring wisdom as they do acquiring gear, they'd probably score a lot better.

So, the next time you feel G.A.S. creeping in, ask yourself: do I really need this club, or do I just need to practice? Because a well-struck ball with an old club beats a brand-new club with a bad swing every single time.

A LITTLE SNACK, A BIG DIFFERENCE

I'VE PLAYED ENOUGH GOLF to know that what you put in your body during a round can make or break your game. A bag full of candy bars and soda might give you a quick boost, but by the back nine, you'll be dragging. The best players I know are intentional about fueling their bodies with the right snacks—some nuts, a banana, maybe a protein bar—something that sustains them over the long haul.

Elijah, one of God's great prophets, found himself in a rough stretch once. He wasn't just tired; he was exhausted, spiritually and physically. He had just faced off against the prophets of Baal, and now, running for his life, he sat under a tree and told God he was done. But God didn't scold him. Instead, He sent an angel with a simple prescription: "Arise and eat." Twice, Elijah was given food and water, and after that, he had the strength to keep going for forty days (1 Kings 19:5-8).

Sometimes, when we're struggling—whether on the course or in life—the best thing we can do is take a moment to rest and refuel. Too often, we try to push through exhaustion, frustration, and discouragement without stopping to consider what we really need. Maybe it's something as simple as better nutrition, or maybe it's stepping aside to take in God's Word and let Him strengthen us.

So next time you're packing your golf bag, think ahead. Bring what will sustain you, not just what sounds good at the moment. And when life gets overwhelming, remember Elijah. Maybe you don't need to quit—maybe you just need a snack.

CHAPTER II

Art of The Swing

"You swing your best when you have the fewest things to think about."
- Bobby Jones

HOLD YOUR POSE

I CAN STILL HEAR MY GOLF COACH saying, "Hold your pose, hold your pose!" He wanted me to finish with my arms high, my chest aimed at the target, and my posture solid until the ball hit the ground. At first, I thought it was just for looks. But there were two real reasons for it.

First, a proper finish means you've made a proper swing. If you're off balance, falling back, or twisting awkwardly, something went wrong in the swing. Holding your finish proves you've stayed in rhythm, that your motion was smooth and complete. Second, it's a reminder that the shot isn't over just because the club has struck the ball. The success of your follow-through is usually proportional to the quality of your ball striking.

Paul had a similar idea when he wrote to the Philippians: "Being confident of this, that He who began a good work in you will carry it on to completion until the day of Christ Jesus" (Philippians 1:6). He was talking about finishing well.

In golf, you don't stop after impact—you finish the motion. In life, it's the same. The Christian life isn't about starting strong and fizzling out. It's about following through, trusting that the work God started in you will be carried to completion—not by your strength, but by His.

A good golfer doesn't just hit the ball and hope. He commits to the whole motion, all the way through. A good

Christian doesn't just start with faith and leave the rest to chance. He trusts, he follows, he finishes.

So, hold your pose. In golf. In life. Finish well. It's the difference between a wild hack and a well-struck shot. And it's the difference between wandering through life and living with purpose.

Fast is Smooth, and Smooth is Fast

I have a little mantra I like to repeat to myself when I'm standing over a shot: *Fast is smooth, and smooth is fast.*

Too many amateur golfers think that if they want to hit the ball far, they need to swing the club as fast as possible. But more often than not, that just leads to a wild slice, a nasty hook, or—if you're really unlucky—a lost ball in the trees. The secret to power in the golf swing isn't just speed— it's *tempo*.

Just think of some of the smoothest swings on tour today —guys like Jake Knapp, Rory McIlroy, or even the great Ernie Els. There's a reason they called him *The Big Easy*. His swing was effortless, fluid, and perfectly balanced. He never looked like he was trying to crush the ball, yet he sent it soaring with seemingly no effort at all.

If you're used to swinging fast, that's fine. But swinging fast *out of tempo* rarely leads to good results. The real key to distance is smoothness. Smooth means controlled. Smooth means rhythm. Smooth means allowing the club to do the work instead of forcing it. Ironically, the best way to produce more speed isn't by swinging harder—it's by swinging *better*.

The same principle applies in life. Rushing, forcing, and trying to power your way through challenges often leads to mistakes. But when you slow down, find your rhythm, and move with purpose, things start to fall into place.

Proverbs 19:2 says, *"Desire without knowledge is not good—how much more will hasty feet miss the way!"* In golf and in life, smooth and steady beats rushed and reckless every time. So the next time you're standing over the ball, take a deep breath, relax, and remember: *Fast is smooth, and smooth is fast.*

FIXING YOUR SLICE

MOST AMATEUR GOLFERS STRUGGLE WITH A SLICE. For a right-handed player, that means the ball starts out straight but then veers sharply to the right. It's frustrating. You aim left to compensate, but the ball still slices right, sometimes worse than before.

A slice happens because of the way you're swinging. Most golfers try to fix it by doing the very thing that *causes* it—coming over the top, swiping across the ball from right to left in a desperate attempt to steer it straight. But golf doesn't work that way.

If you really want to stop slicing, you have to do something that feels completely wrong. You have to swing *to the right*. That's what they call an "inside-out" path. It's the only way to create the spin that straightens the ball out—or even makes it draw a little left. It feels counterintuitive, but it's the only way to fix the problem.

Life works the same way. The world tells us to follow our instincts, to trust ourselves, to take control. But the Bible teaches that our instincts often lead us the wrong way.

Jesus said the weak are strong. The humble are exalted. The last become first. It's the opposite of what we think, but it's how God's kingdom works.

Proverbs 3:5-6 says it clearly: *"Trust in the Lord with all your heart and lean not on your own understanding; in all your ways submit to him, and he will make your paths straight."*

Next time you're on the course, and that slice starts creeping back into your game, remember—the fix might feel wrong, but it's actually right. And in life, don't just go with your gut—trust God's way instead.

The Stroke That Counts

How many times have you or a friend stepped up to the tee, taken a few waggles, and accidentally knocked the ball off the tee? Everyone grins, and someone jokes, *"That's one stroke!"* But we all know better. According to the Rules of Golf, an accidental nudge doesn't count as a stroke.

But here's something surprising—if you take a full swing and completely miss, that does count. Rule 10.1a states:

> *"A stroke is the forward movement of the club made to strike the ball."*

That means even if the ball never moves, your attempt alone is counted. The heart of the rule isn't in the ball moving—it's in your intention to hit it.

That's a lesson in life and faith. Many people assume that being a Christian is about the big, visible things—what gets done, what can be measured. But God looks deeper. Our faith is counted by our intention, but proven by our follow-through.

James 2:17 says it plainly; *"So also faith by itself, if it does not have works, is dead."*

It's one thing to say you believe, to have a heart that desires to follow Christ. But just like a golf swing, intention alone isn't enough. You have to connect. You have to follow through.

So next time you're on the tee and you accidentally knock the ball off, take a breath—that wasn't your intention. But when you swing, commit. Move forward with purpose, both in your golf game and in your walk with Christ. Because in both, it's not just about good intentions—it's about taking action in faith.

Start Your Day Like a Champion

The best golfers in the world don't just step up and hit the ball. They follow a routine—the same steps every time. Pick a target. Visualize the shot. Take a couple of practice swings. Deep breath. And go.

Virtually every top golfer—Tiger Woods, Jack Nicklaus, Rory McIlroy—has a set pre-shot routine. Each one is different, unique to the player, but it serves the same purpose. It's a ritual that helps them calm down, build consistency, and handle pressure when it matters most.

Most amateurs? They just walk up and swing, hoping for the best. Sometimes it works, but more often, it doesn't. A pre-shot routine builds consistency, helps with focus, and keeps the nerves in check.

The Christian life is shockingly similar. If you roll out of bed and rush into the day without preparing your heart, you're swinging blind. But if you take the time to start with prayer, scripture, and quiet time with the Lord, you're setting yourself up for success—just like a good pre-shot routine sets you up for a better swing.

Jesus Himself did this. Mark 1:35 says, *"Very early in the morning, while it was still dark, Jesus got up, left the house and went off to a solitary place, where he prayed."* If Jesus needed time alone with the Father before stepping into the demands of the day, how much more do we?

So before you tee off in the morning—both in golf and in life—take the time to prepare. Find your quiet place. Set your mind on the right target. Breathe. Pray. Then go.

HIT DOWN ON IT!

A COMMON MISTAKE AMONG US AMATEUR GOLFERS is trying to help the ball into the air. We swing up on it, thinking that's the way to get height. But the truth is, to make the ball rise, you've got to hit down.

A well-struck iron shot happens when the club face compresses the ball against the turf with a descending blow. That compression creates backspin, which lifts the ball into the air naturally. The club is designed that way. But when a golfer tries to 'help' the ball by scooping it, they actually work against the club's design—and the results aren't pretty. Thin shots that barely leave the ground, weak pop-ups that land well short, or divots so big you feel like you should put up a "ground under repair" sign.

The Christian life isn't so different. God designed us to worship Him, to walk humbly, and to trust Him. But too often, we try to "help" God by working our way into His good graces, thinking that if we just do enough good things, we'll elevate ourselves spiritually. That's like trying to scoop the ball into the air instead of striking it the way it was designed.

Proverbs 3:5-6 reminds us, *"Trust in the Lord with all your heart and lean not on your own understanding; in all your ways submit to him, and he will make your paths straight."* The key is humility—trusting that God's way works, even when it feels counterintuitive.

So, the next time you're standing over the ball, remember: hit down to go up. Trust the design. Swing with confidence. And in life, humble yourself before God—He'll take care of the lift.

Hold The Baby Bird

IF YOU VISIT JUST ABOUT ANY GOLF COURSE in America, you'll notice that nearly every golfer is wearing a glove. Ask them why, and most will tell you it's to prevent blisters or calluses. But that's not really the reason at all. The real purpose of a golf glove is to help you maintain a secure grip so you don't have to hold the club too tightly.

One of the quickest ways to sabotage your swing is by gripping the club like you're trying to wring water from a towel. A grip that's too tight robs you of both power and control. In fact, it's a major cause of that frustrating slice. Sam Snead, one of the greatest ball strikers of all time, put it best when he said you should hold the club like you would hold a baby bird—*"firm enough so it won't fly away, but gentle enough so you don't crush it."*

That's good advice for golf—and for life. Too often, we hold onto things too tightly—our possessions, our plans, even our relationships—thinking that if we just keep a firm enough grasp, we can control the outcome. But life doesn't work that way. If you grip too hard, you're likely to squeeze the life right out of what you love.

The Bible speaks to this in Matthew 6:19-21:

"Do not lay up for yourselves treasures on earth, where moth and rust destroy and where thieves break in and steal, but lay up for yourselves treasures in heaven... For where your treasure is, there your heart will be also."

Jesus reminds us that our grip should be loose when it comes to the temporary things of this world. Just as a tight grip in golf can ruin a good swing, clinging too tightly to the things of this life can keep us from trusting God fully. The best golf shots—and the best lives—come from holding things loosely, letting God guide the outcome.

Think About It:

What's something in your life that you may be gripping too tightly instead of trusting God with?

CLUB SELECTION MATTERS

ONE TIME EARLY IN MY LIFE as a new golfer, I stepped up

to the hole, 120 yards to the pin, feeling confident. I reached into my bag, pulled out what I thought was my nine iron, and took my stance. My grip felt good, my swing was solid, and the ball soared into the sky—a beautiful shot. But as I watched it fly high over the pin, clear the green, and disappear into the woods behind it, I realized something was wrong.

Turns out, I hadn't grabbed my nine iron—I'd grabbed my six iron! My first set of clubs didn't have an underline on the numbers, so my six and my nine looked exactly the same. A simple mistake, but one that made all the difference.

That day, I learned an important lesson: club selection is critical. Once you know the distance, you have to pick the right tool for the shot—then trust it. A perfect swing with the wrong club won't get you the result you want.

In a similar way, God has given us different "clubs" to use in different situations—patience, boldness, gentleness, even righteous anger when necessary. The key is knowing which one to pull from the bag. If you swing with anger when the moment calls for patience, you might do more harm than good. If you hesitate when you should be bold, you might miss an opportunity.

Ecclesiastes 3:1 reminds us:

"For everything there is a season, and a time for every matter under heaven."

A wise golfer knows his clubs. A wise man knows when to speak, when to listen, when to stand firm, and when to yield. The next time you're facing a challenge, don't just grab the first club you see. Take a moment. Read the situation. Then make your swing with confidence.

Hitting the Sweet Spot

I'll never forget one of my early lessons in golf. I was out on the range, still an beginner in every sense of the word, trying to make solid contact. Then, it happened—I hit a shot so pure, it felt effortless. My coach grinned and said, "You really hit that one on the screws."

I had no idea what he meant. Screws? My club didn't have any.

Later that day, he walked me into the clubhouse and pulled out an old persimmon wood. Right there on the face of the club were a set of screws, marking the sweet spot—the place where a perfectly struck shot transfers the most energy to the ball with the least resistance. Even though modern clubs don't have those screws anymore, the phrase stuck around. Every golfer knows the feeling of flushing a shot, and it all comes down to hitting the sweet spot.

Life has a sweet spot, too. As Christians, we experience it when we're living right in the center of God's will—when our heart, mind, and actions align with His purpose.

Romans 12:2 reminds us not to conform to the world but to be transformed by the renewing of our mind, so that we can "test and approve what God's will is—his good, pleasing, and perfect will."

Just like in golf, when you hit life's sweet spot, things don't feel forced. There's peace, purpose, and a sense that you're right where you're meant to be. It doesn't mean life is easy—just like golf, you'll still have to adjust for wind, lie, and hazards—but when you're surrendered daily to God, you'll find the best contact, the purest joy, and the most impact.

⛳

The Ten-Finger Grip

Sometimes called "the baseball grip," the ten-finger grip is my go-to for new players, especially younger ones and beginners. While you won't see it much on the PGA Tour, there are some clear advantages. First, it puts the club in contact with the fingers rather than the palms. That's why "baseball grip" is actually a bit misleading—because in baseball, the bat is gripped more with the palms. In golf, using the fingers allows for more whip, more feel, and ultimately more speed.

Second, the ten-finger grip feels natural. If you hand a child a golf club and ask them to swing, they won't instinctively interlock or overlap their fingers like an experienced golfer—they'll grip it with all ten fingers, because that's what feels right.

It's also a great grip for juniors and women. For those with smaller hands, an interlocking or overlapping grip can feel unnatural, even restrictive. The ten-finger grip allows for better control and a more secure hold, helping these players develop confidence and a smooth swing.

Faith works much the same way. Sometimes, we try to force ourselves into practices that feel unnatural, assuming they will make us "more spiritual." We think we need complex prayers, rigid disciplines, or a long history of church knowledge to grow in faith. But Jesus said, *"Truly, I tell you, whoever does not receive the kingdom of God like a little child will never enter it" (Luke 18:17).*

A child's grip on the club is simple and instinctive—just like a child's trust in God. When we approach Him with faith that is unhindered by overcomplication, we allow ourselves to truly grow.

KEEP YOUR HEAD DOWN? MAYBE NOT.

WHEN I FIRST STARTED GOLFING, I hit a lot of thin shots —those frustrating little skimmers that barely get off the ground. After one particularly ugly topper that scurried about 75 yards but never got higher than my knees, I sighed and muttered, *"Lifted my head again."*

My coach shook his head. *"Maybe you lifted your head,"* he said, *"but that's not your problem. You're trying to scoop it."*

I thought I knew what I had done wrong—but I was the one swinging the club. I couldn't really see my own mistake. My coach could. He had a clearer view of what was happening and offered the correction I needed.

I still hear golfers say they topped a shot because they lifted their head. But the real issue is usually how the club meets the ball. A topped shot happens when the clubface strikes the ball on the way up, hitting it above the equator. This creates topspin and that dreaded low, bouncing trajectory—just like a ping-pong shot with too much forward spin.

If you're struggling with topping the ball, here are two things to try: First, focus on hitting *down* on the shot. Make a divot. Picture yourself driving the ball into the turf just an inch or two ahead of where it sits. That helps to ensures a descending blow instead of an upward scoop. And if that doesn't work, a short-term fix might be to move the ball back in your stance by half a ball or so. This helps you make contact with the lower part of the ball.

If you do that right, chances are your head will stay where it needs to. But even if it doesn't, the ball doesn't care what your head is doing—just what the club is doing when it meets the ball. If you still have problems, have someone with some experience take a look at your swing to help you evaluate the problem.

We often assume we know our struggles, but our perspective is limited. We need godly people around us—friends, mentors, pastors—who can see what we can't and speak truth into our lives. Proverbs 27:6 says, *"Wounds from a friend can be trusted, but an enemy multiplies kisses."* A true friend, like my coach, doesn't just tell us what we want to hear; they tell us what we need to hear.

CHAPTER III

Practice Makes Progress

"The more I practice, the luckier I get."
- Gary Player (and others)

Practice Like You Play

MY GOLF COACH HAD ONE RULE ON THE RANGE—never hit the same club too many times in a row. If I wanted to groove my seven iron, he'd let me take a handful of swings, but then he'd make me switch. Driver, then iron, then wedge, then back again.

I didn't like it at first. I wanted to find my rhythm, dial in my swing. But he would just shake his head and say, *"You have to practice the way you play."*

He was right. There's no scenario on the course where you get to hit the same club ten times in a row. Golf isn't about perfecting one shot—it's about adapting, adjusting, and executing whatever shot is needed next. The way you practice has to prepare you for the real thing.

Faith works the same way. It's not enough to just know the right thing to do—we have to put it into action. James 1:22 says, *"Do not merely listen to the word, and so deceive yourselves. Do what it says."*

Plenty of golfers look great on the range but struggle on the course. And plenty of people hear the truth of God's Word but never apply it to their lives. Both are making the same mistake—they're practicing, but they're not preparing.

So the next time you head to the range, mix it up. Practice the way you play. And in life, don't just *hear* the truth—live it.

Practice Swing Syndrome

Have you ever played with someone who takes too many practice swings? I call it *PSS—Practice Swing Syndrome*. I've got a buddy who will take five or six practice swings before every shot. And I'll admit, they look pretty good—nice rhythm, solid motion. But when it comes time to actually hit the ball? Well, that's a different story. It's a completely different swing.

If you watch the pros, you'll notice something: they don't usually take full practice swings. Maybe they'll rehearse a takeaway in slow motion or brush the grass with a little half-swing before a chip. But you won't see them standing over the ball, grinding through five or six rehearsals.

There's a reason for that. Besides making the game drag on, a practice swing is mostly useless if you don't have a target—no ball, no focus.

In golf, only one thing matters: making solid contact with the ball. So if you must take a practice swing, make it count. Take one—just one—and give yourself a target. Pick out a blade of grass or a speck of dirt where the ball would be. Then step up, settle in, and make a confident swing with your full focus on your actual target—the ball.

The same is true in our spiritual life. Some people spend all their time preparing—reading books, listening to sermons, even making plans—but they never take action.

James 1:22 says, *"Do not merely listen to the word, and so deceive yourselves. Do what it says."* At some point, faith requires action.

God didn't call us to take endless practice swings. He calls us to step forward, trust Him, and take the shot. So don't be afraid to commit—whether in golf or in your walk with God. Swing with purpose, trust the process, and let God take care of the results.

⛳

Warming Up Without Wearing Out

Should you warm up? Yes. Should you overdo it? No!

I've seen many golfers walk straight from the parking lot to the first tee, stiff as a board, and wonder why their first drive looks like a wounded duck. I've also seen players beat balls on the range until they've got nothing left for the round. Both are mistakes.

The purpose of a warm-up is twofold: to loosen up and to find your tempo. The fluidity of your swing depends on how relaxed your muscles are, and the older we get, the harder that becomes. So before you even take a swing, stretch. Loosen your back, your shoulders, your legs. Golf is a game of rhythm, not rigidity.

When you do start hitting balls, resist the urge to grab your driver and start swinging for the fences. Instead, take a short iron—maybe a nine or a pitching wedge—and hit a few easy shots off a tee. No digging it out of the dirt, no forcing it. Just find your tempo. When your body and your rhythm feel right, you're ready.

And don't overdo it. Ten or fifteen shots is plenty. The goal isn't to win the range session—it's to prepare for the round. A tired golfer makes bad swings, and bad swings make long rounds.

Paul said it well in 1 Corinthians 9:25—*"Everyone who competes in the games exercises self-control in all things."* Preparation matters, but so does self-control. If you warm up the right way, you'll step onto the first tee loose, confident, and ready. And in golf, as in faith, it's not about how hard you start—it's about being steady all the way through.

Changing Putters

I just bought another putter. It's not new, of course —just a used one I found for a fraction of the price. Since I started golfing some 15+ years ago, I've probably cycled through five or six putters. You'll notice a lot of tour players doing the same. A few bad rounds, and suddenly that putter is banished to the garage or donated to charity. Then they find a new one, only to eventually move on from that, too.

It's not just putters either—there's always some new grip method floating around. Left-hand low, claw grip, arm lock—golfers will try just about anything to see if it'll give them an edge on the greens.

Now, I'm not saying there's anything wrong with testing out new equipment or trying a different grip. But at some point, it might say more about our confidence than our tools. Tiger Woods has technically used a couple of different putters, but if you lined them up, you'd see they're nearly identical. Custom-built for him, the differences are minute—millimeters here, a slight adjustment there.

Constantly switching putters reminds me a lot of how people approach their faith. Some are always looking for the "perfect" church, the perfect Bible translation, the perfect devotional method—thinking that if they just find the right tool, their faith will suddenly feel effortless. But more often than not, the problem isn't the tool. It's the trust in it.

Faith, like putting, thrives on consistency and commitment. If we're always chasing the latest and greatest, we'll never settle in and actually grow. That said, sometimes a change is necessary—not as a quick fix, but as a fresh perspective. A new study method, a different way of praying, or even a shift in our surroundings can bring renewal. The key is knowing whether we're making a meaningful adjustment or just chasing the next thing, hoping it'll be the answer.

Think About It: Are you constantly searching for the next new thing in your faith, hoping it will suddenly make everything easier? Or are you committed to steady growth, trusting that consistency and faithfulness will lead to real transformation?

Practicing Like the Pros

Next time a professional golf tournament comes to town, do yourself a favor—skip the tournament ticket and attend a practice round instead.

Practice rounds are usually much cheaper than tournament days, and the crowds are smaller, which means you can get up close to the action. You'll not only see the best players in the world, but you'll hear them—talking through shots with their caddies, strategizing about angles, wind, and slopes. It's like watching a master class in course management.

Practice Makes Progress

One of the most eye-opening things about a practice round is that pros don't play it like a regular round. They're not keeping score. Instead, they hit different shots from different locations—chip from a tricky lie, work the ball left and right, test different approaches to the green. They use the course itself as their practice ground, not just the range.

Most amateur golfers could learn a lesson from this. Practice doesn't have to be confined to the range. If you're out on the course when it's not crowded, take a few extra shots from different spots. Try shaping the ball. Hit a second chip. Experiment with different clubs around the green. Instead of just playing holes, practice shots that will actually help you score better.

The pros know something that amateurs often forget—real improvement happens when you prepare for the situations you'll actually face.

The same is true in life and faith. Proverbs 22:3 says, "The prudent sees danger and hides himself, but the simple go on and suffer for it." Wise people prepare for the challenges ahead, while the foolish charge forward without considering what's coming. A golfer who never practices tough shots will struggle when they face them in a tournament. Likewise, a person who never prepares their heart and mind with Scripture, prayer, and wise counsel will find themselves overwhelmed when life's difficulties arise.

So don't just go through the motions. Be intentional

about preparing for what's ahead. In golf and in life, your preparation today determines your success tomorrow.

The Short Game of Faith

If you want to practice your driver, you almost certainly have to go to the driving range, the golf course, or maybe a simulator. Same for practicing your irons or even your sand shots. But the easiest part of your game to practice—the short game—can be done in your backyard, your living room, or just about anywhere.

It's amazing how few of us actually practice this part of the game, considering we'll hit more shots on and around the green than any other place during a round. Yet, the challenge of practicing at home is simple—it's kinda boring. We like the big, booming drives. We want the excitement. But good golfers know that making up little games—hitting a bucket in the backyard, rolling putts to a coin on the carpet—keeps practice interesting and makes a real difference in your score.

Spiritual life is a lot like that. We love the big, exciting moments—the mountain-top experiences, the revivals, the big decisions. But most of our faith is lived in the short game—small moments of prayer, quiet obedience, little acts of kindness. Those moments may not seem thrilling, but they're what shape us over time. And just like chipping and putting, faith grows stronger when we make a habit of practicing it daily.

The question is—do you have a way to make it interesting? Maybe it's keeping a prayer journal and seeing how God answers over time. Maybe it's memorizing a verse a week with a friend. Whatever it is, find a way to practice the small things, because just like in golf, the short game is where the real victories are won.

Think About it:

What's one small, daily habit in your spiritual life—prayer, Scripture reading, kindness—that you tend to overlook because it doesn't feel exciting? How can you make it more engaging so you actually practice it?

CHAPTER IV

Honesty Is The Best Policy

"*The real test of a man's character
is what he does when no one is watching.*"
— John Wooden

KEEP AN HONEST SCORE

IT DOESN'T MATTER TOO MUCH IF YOU KEEP SCORE when you play golf. Some days, it's best just to enjoy the walk, the fresh air, and the time with friends. But if you *do* keep score, do it the right way.

I've played with guys who claim to shoot in the 70s or 80s, but when you actually watch them play, you realize they only *sort of* keep score. They give themselves putts they didn't make. They ignore penalties. They take an extra shot or two and don't write it down.

Here's the problem: if you don't keep an honest score, you'll never really know if you're improving. For example, if you hit a ball out of bounds, you have to go back and hit again . If you don't, your score means nothing.

A man is only as good as his word. If you say you're going to do something, then do it. But don't commit to something you know you can't follow through on. Jesus said it best: *"Let your 'Yes' be 'Yes,' and your 'No,' 'No.'" (Matthew 5:37)*

So next time you're out on the course, if you just want to have fun, great—don't worry about the score. But if you keep score, be honest about it. Play the game the right way. Because how you handle small things, even something as simple as counting strokes, says a lot about your character.

Play It as It Lies

The other day, I was golfing with a friend when we both hit perfect drives—right down the middle of the fairway. But when we walked up to our balls, he saw that his had settled in a divot.

Without hesitation, he reached down to move it.

"What are you doing?" I asked.

He looked at me and said, "I should be rewarded for hitting a perfect drive."

I agreed with him—he *should* be rewarded. But golf isn't always fair. It's a game of skill and chance, and sometimes, no matter how well you play, you end up in a bad spot.

Bobby Jones put it best: *"Golf is the closest game to the game we call life. You get bad breaks from good shots; you get good breaks from bad shots—but you have to play the ball where it lies."*

The game's integrity depends on that. Moving the ball would have made his next shot easier, but it wouldn't have made him a better golfer. The challenge of hitting out of the divot is what makes the game meaningful.

Life works the same way. Sometimes, you do everything right—work hard, make good decisions, treat people well—and still find yourself in a tough spot. It's tempting to want to change the rules, to find a way around the hardship. But facing challenges head-on builds character.

James put it this way: *"Consider it pure joy, my brothers and sisters, whenever you face trials of many kinds, because you know that the testing of your faith produces perseverance."* (James 1:2-3)

Life has its divots. You might not deserve them, but they're there just the same. And if you learn to play the ball as it lies, you'll come out stronger on the other side.

Golf Meltdowns & Moving Forward

GOLF IS A GAME OF CONTROL—controlling your swing, your emotions, and your decisions. But sometimes, no matter how well you prepare, the game gets away from you. Just ask Jordan Spieth.

At the 2016 Masters, Spieth looked untouchable. Heading into the back nine on Sunday, he had a five-shot lead. Then came Amen Corner. A bogey on 10. A bogey on 11. And then, disaster on 12—a chunked wedge into Rae's Creek, followed by another. A quadruple-bogey seven. In just three holes, the green jacket slipped off his shoulders.

We've all been there, maybe not at Augusta, but on our own courses. A couple of bad swings, a lost ball, a string of double bogeys—and suddenly, frustration takes over. The round that started so well unravels, and we have a choice to make: let it ruin the day, or reset and move forward.

The Bible reminds us that failure isn't final. Psalm 37:23-24 says, *"The Lord makes firm the steps of the one who delights in him; though he may stumble, he will not fall, for the Lord upholds him with his hand."*

Spieth could have let that Masters collapse define him, but he didn't. He bounced back, worked on his game, and won the Open Championship the following year.

Bad holes happen. Bad days happen. But what matters most is what you do next. When your round goes south, take a deep breath. Slow down. Refocus. And remember—golf, like life, isn't about avoiding mistakes. It's about learning from them and moving forward.

YOU'RE NOT GOOD ENOUGH TO GET MAD!

AFTER ABOUT A YEAR AND A HALF OF LESSONS, I started to see some real improvement in my game. I could hit the ball straighter, and on a good day, I'd make par about half the time. It felt like I was finally getting somewhere.

One afternoon, my coach and I were playing a few holes

when I hit a tee shot so far out of bounds it might as well have had a passport. Frustrated, I slammed my club into the ground. My coach didn't say anything right away—just watched as I stewed. Then, with a little grin, he said, *"Take it easy, Phil. You're not good enough to get mad."*

I'll admit, that stung a little. But he was right. What was I so upset about? I wasn't on the PGA Tour. I wasn't competing for a paycheck. I was just a guy trying to get better at a game.

I've seen plenty of golfers throw fits—slamming clubs, tossing them into lakes, even snapping them over their knees. But the truth is, if you can't control your temper on the course, chances are you struggle with it off the course too. Golf has a funny way of revealing your character.

Self-control is one of the core values of Christianity. The Bible tells us that patience and discipline are marks of a mature believer. Proverbs 16:32 says, *"Better a patient person than a warrior, one with self-control than one who takes a city."* If a bad shot is enough to send you into a blind rage, maybe it's not just your swing that needs work.

The Price of Integrity

GOLF IS A FUNNY GAME. You can spend years trying to fix a slice, finally get it straightened out, and then wake up one morning hitting a hook instead. You can hit the ball flush on the range, only to thin it across the green when it counts. But there's one thing golf demands beyond skill: honesty.

In the 2024 Tour Championship, Sahith Theegala faced a moment most folks will never experience—because most folks will never be in a position to lose $2.5 million over a sliver of sand. After finding a bunker, Theegala took his backswing and felt—just barely—his club graze the sand. No one saw it. The cameras couldn't even pick it up. But he felt it.

The rules of golf are clear. Rule 12.2b says touching the sand on a practice swing or backswing is a penalty. So, Theegala did what most wouldn't. He called in an official, explained what he thought had happened, and took the penalty. That stroke could have been the difference between second place and third, between a bigger check and a smaller one. And yet, he never hesitated.

No one else would have known. But he would have.

Proverbs 28:6 says, "Better is a poor man who walks in his integrity than a rich man who is crooked in his ways." In the end, Theegala walked away with $7.5 million instead of $10 million, but more importantly, he walked away with his honor intact. And when he looks in the mirror, he won't see a man who bent the rules to get ahead. He'll see a man who did what was right when no one was looking.

Golf has a way of revealing what kind of person you really are. It's not just about how well you hit a drive or roll a putt—it's about the decisions you make when no one's watching.

Don't Ask for a Gimme

I WAS PLAYING MATCH PLAY GOLF WITH A FRIEND, hole by hole, each worth a point. We got to the green, and he rolled his putt up to about three and a half feet. He looked at me and said, "Aren't you going to give me that?"

Now, in match play, you can concede a putt. It's called a "gimme"—a way of saying, *I trust you'd make that anyway, so let's move on.* But a gimme is just that—a *give* me, not a *take* me. You should never ask for one. It's poor etiquette, and frankly, it's a little pitiful. Asking for a gimme is basically admitting you don't think you can make it.

I think about that in faith. Sometimes we pray for things as if we're looking for a handout rather than stepping up with confidence in what God has already equipped us to do. We want an easy answer, a shortcut, or a guarantee of success before we even take the shot. But faith doesn't work like that.

James 2:17 says, *"Faith by itself, if it is not accompanied by action, is dead."* Faith isn't about waiting for everything to be handed to you. It's about trusting God enough to step up and take the putt.

Sure, sometimes God grants a gimme—an unexpected blessing, an open door we didn't see coming. But we shouldn't go through life asking for them. Instead, we step up, line up the putt, and put our faith into action.

The Handicap of Grace

One of the more unique aspects of golf is the handicap system. In a world where certain words carry a stigma, "handicap" might sound like a drawback—but in golf, it's actually a benefit, designed to make the game more balanced and inclusive. A handicap allows golfers of all skill levels to compete on an even playing field.

A lot of people think a handicap is just your average score, but that's not quite right. It's actually a calculation of your best rounds, factoring in the difficulty of the course. In other words, it's a measure of how many strokes you'd need, on your best day, to shoot even par.

At the time of writing this, I carry a 10.9 handicap, which means that on my best day, I'd still need nearly 11 strokes to reach par on a typical course. If I were to play against a scratch golfer—someone who needs no extra strokes—the handicap system levels the field. It makes the game fair, no matter who's playing.

And that, my friend, is the message of grace.

See, in the grand tournament of life, none of us measure up to God's standard. If this were golf, Jesus would shoot 18 under every time. Perfect score, every round. No mistakes, no mulligans, no bogeys. Meanwhile, the rest of us? We're hacking it out of the rough, losing balls in the water, and racking up double bogeys.

But here's the beauty of grace—Jesus gives us His scorecard. Through His sacrifice, He evens the playing field. His perfection covers our imperfection. His righteousness allows us to stand before God, not based on our own performance, but on His.

Without a handicap, most of us wouldn't stand a chance on the golf course. Without grace, none of us would stand a chance before God.

But thanks be to Christ, we don't have to.

CHAPTER V

The Scoring Game

"It doesn't matter where you hit the drive if you make the putt."
- Seve Ballesteros

PUTT YOUR WAY TO WISDOM

ARNOLD PALMER ONCE SAID, "Your best chip is rarely better than your worst putt." That's a lesson many amateurs learn the hard way. They find themselves a few paces off the green, sitting in the fringe, and think, *I'll just chip this close to the pin.* But more often than not, they misjudge it—maybe they chili-dip it short or send it skidding across the green. Meanwhile, the simple, steady putt would have left them in better shape.

I have a friend, an excellent golfer with about an eight handicap, who putts almost everything around the green. Unless he's completely buried in thick grass, the putter is his go-to club. Other guys in our group give him a hard time about it, but when the scorecards are tallied, he's usually the one coming out ahead.

Here's what I tell my students: Don't be afraid to use the putter from the fringe—a shot often facetiously called the "Texas wedge." If the ground is smooth and the path is clear, keeping the ball on the ground gives you the most control. The fancy shot isn't always the smartest shot.

It's the same in life. Sometimes, the simplest option—the one that seems too obvious or even counterintuitive—is actually the best one. Forgiving someone who wronged you might not make sense to others. They might say you're being weak, that you should get even. But forgiveness, like using the Texas wedge, often leads to a far better outcome. *"Bear with each other and forgive one another if any of you has a grievance against someone. Forgive as the Lord forgave you"* (*Colossians 3:13*).

Let the other guys chip if they want. You just take the steady path and putt your way to something better.

⛳

Let It Die at the Hole

A LOT OF GOLF INSTRUCTORS WILL TELL YOU that the ideal pace for a putt is one that, if missed, rolls about 17 inches past the hole. Now, I'm no golf scientist, but in my experience, that approach can lead to a lot of trouble.

There are two big risks with hitting a putt too firm. First, if the ball has too much pace and catches the edge, it's bound to lip out instead of dropping. A putt that might have fallen with softer speed ends up spinning away. Second, if you miss altogether, you're left with a stressful comeback putt. Instead of a tap-in, you're standing over a tricky four-footer, suddenly feeling the pressure.

Like the great Harvey Penick, I prefer a putt that dies at or near the hole. I know some coaches live by the old saying, *"Never up, never in."* But I think a dying putt gives you two big advantages: First, A slow-moving ball has a better chance of falling in. A putt with just enough speed to reach the hole has more room to drop than one racing past. Second, If it doesn't fall, it's an easy tap-in. No stress, no long comebacker, just a simple finish.

This principle applies beyond golf, too. Proverbs 19:2 says, *"Desire without knowledge is not good—how much more will hasty feet miss the way!"* Sometimes in life, we rush ahead with too much force—too much urgency—and we miss opportunities that a more measured approach might have captured. Patience and precision often lead to better results than speed and aggression.

So next time you're on the green, don't fire your putt at the hole like it's a cannon shot. Let it die at the cup. And in life, remember—the right pace is just as important as the right direction.

THE AGONY OF THE THREE-PUTT

THERE MAY BE NO WORSE FEELING IN GOLF than walking off a green with a three-putt. You did all the hard work—found the fairway, hit a solid approach, maybe even gave yourself a look at birdie. And then, somehow, you needed three strokes with the flat stick to finish the job. It doesn't seem fair.

The problem with three-putting is that it gets in your head. Miss the first putt, and suddenly you're thinking about not three-putting. You get tentative, afraid of running it past. Or you get aggressive, trying to make up for the mistake, and shove the next one five feet by. Either way, you've turned a simple task into a mental battle.

But here's the thing: Three-putts don't usually happen because of the last putt. They happen because of the first one. Maybe you misread the slope, maybe you left yourself too much work, maybe you just weren't fully committed. Whatever the case, once that first putt goes wrong, you're scrambling.

Funny how similar that is to life. We don't usually end up in a mess because of one big mistake. It's often the small missteps along the way—a rushed decision, an unwise word, a moment of distraction—that put us in a tough spot. That's why Proverbs 4:26 says, *"Give careful thought to the paths for your feet and be steadfast in all your ways."* Small choices matter. If you want to avoid trouble, pay attention to the first step, not just the last one.

So, the next time you face a long putt, don't just hope to avoid a three-putt. Commit to the first stroke. Read it well, trust your line, and give it the right pace. And in life, don't wait until you're in trouble to make a good decision. Start strong, and you'll finish well.

Start Small, Win Big

When I was teaching golf to juniors, I always started them on the green with a putter. No drivers, no long irons—just putting. Once they got comfortable with that, we'd move to chipping. I made it fun, setting up little games and rewarding them with colorful golf balls, funny tees, or candy when they did well. Only after they had a feel for the short game did we work our way back to irons, and eventually, the driver.

Most people do the opposite. They grab a driver first and try to launch the ball as far as possible. But anyone who's played golf for a while knows the truth: it's the *small stuff* that matters most.

Nearly half the shots in a round of golf happen with the putter. And if you're like most amateurs, you'll spend plenty of time chipping around the green, trying to save strokes. Yet, this is the part of the game most people ignore or dismiss. They want to crush 300-yard drives, but the players who win? They're the ones who master the little shots.

A lot of people dream about changing the world, making a big impact, leaving a legacy. But real change doesn't start with the big stuff—it starts small. How you treat your family. How you speak to your friends. How you love your neighbor.

Jesus put it this way: *"Whoever is faithful in the little things will also be faithful in much."* (Luke 16:10)

In golf and in life, the little things matter more than you think. Take care of them, and the big things will take care of themselves.

Keep Your Eyes Off The Target?

When it comes to chipping from off the green, the best advice I ever got was this: *Don't look at the flag!* That might sound strange at first—after all, the flag marks the target. But if you focus only on the hole, you're missing the key to a good chip shot.

The secret to a solid chip isn't aiming at the flag—it's knowing where to *land* the ball. A well-played chip shot starts with picking the right landing spot, considering how the ball will roll after it touches down. The best players don't just think about where they want the ball to finish; they focus on the first point of contact with the green and trust their touch to do the rest.

I learned this the hard way. Early on, I aimed my chips straight at the flag, hoping they'd settle right next to the cup. More often than not, they didn't. The ball would land too far, roll too much, and end up well past my target. Over time, I realized that success in chipping—like success in life—is about focusing on the *next right step*, not just the end goal.

There are plenty of factors at play—the smoothness of the green, the slope, the type of lie you're hitting from—but one thing is certain: if you're only looking at the flag, you're likely sending your ball too far. The better approach is to pick a landing spot, trust your touch, and let the ball do the rest.

Life's a lot like that. Sometimes we get so fixated on the end result—where we *want* to be—that we forget about the steps it takes to get there. But just like in golf, wisdom teaches us to focus on the next right move, trusting that God will take care of the roll.

Good Good?

If you're a golfer under 50, chances are you've heard of *Good Good*. It's a group of guys who make YouTube videos about golf—having fun, competing, and showing that the game is as much about camaraderie as it is about skill. I admit it—I love watching them as much as the next guy.

But the phrase *Good Good* actually comes from something you might hear on the course. If two players both have putts inside a reasonable range, one might look at the other and say, *"Good Good?"* It's an offer: *I'll give you your putt if you give me mine.* A mutual concession. A handshake deal based on trust.

And that's the key—*trust*. You wouldn't throw out a *Good Good* to just anyone. You have to believe the other person will reciprocate. Every good compromise is built on trust. And in the Christian life, trust is the foundation of accountability.

Proverbs 27:17 says, *"As iron sharpens iron, so one person sharpens another."* But that sharpening can only happen if there's trust—if you've put in the time, built the relationship, and proven that you have each other's best interests at heart.

Accountability isn't about handing out judgment; it's about standing alongside someone, knowing that when they give you the truth, it's for your good. And when you do the same, they'll receive it the same way. Just like on the course, you don't call *Good Good* with a stranger. You call it with someone you trust.

CHAPTER VI

Life on The Fairway

"Mistakes are part of the game. It's how well
you recover from them,
that's the mark of a great player."
- Alice Cooper

PILGRIM'S RUN

MY FAVORITE GOLF COURSE in the whole world is *Pilgrim's Run*, nestled about 30 minutes north of Grand Rapids, Michigan. If heaven has a front nine, I imagine it looks something like this—rolling fairways winding through a boreal forest, pristine tee boxes, and greens that test your faith but reward the faithful.

But what makes *Pilgrim's Run* special to me isn't just the scenery or the pristine conditions. It's the meaning behind the name. The course is inspired by *The Pilgrim's Progress*, John Bunyan's classic allegory about a man's journey from sin to salvation. Christian, the main character, faces trials, pitfalls, and unexpected obstacles, but with perseverance and faith, he ultimately reaches the Celestial City.

If that doesn't sound like a round of golf, I don't know what does.

It all starts at *Pleasant Arbor*—which feels like an encouraging beginning. But don't get too comfortable, because hole two is *Difficulty*, and by hole three, you're knee-deep in the *Slough of Despond*, wondering why you ever thought this game was fun. The names alone tell the story. Hole seven? *Bottomless Pit*—a 191 yard par 3 that plays downhill over a deep Vally. By the back nine, you face *Giant Despair*, *Dark Valley*, and *Valley of Humility*—all of which describe my state of mind when my approach shot plugs in a bunker.

But just like in the book, perseverance matters. Keep pressing on, and you'll find yourself on *Straight Way*, walking the *Narrow Way*, and finishing strong at *Entice*—a fitting name for 18, because no matter how bad your round went, you're already thinking about coming back for another one.

Golf, like faith, requires perseverance. You'll face hazards, bad bounces, and days when you wonder why you ever picked up a club in the first place. But stay the course, keep your eyes on the goal, and trust that the next shot is always an opportunity for redemption. As Paul reminds us, *"But one thing I do: Forgetting what is behind and straining toward what is ahead, I press on toward the goal to win the prize for which God has called me heavenward in Christ Jesus."* (Philippians 3:13-14).

Or in this case, forget that double on *Vainglory*, and keep moving forward—trusting that there's always a way to get up and down.

And if you ever do make it to *Pilgrim's Run*, take my advice: Avoid the bunkers on the par 3 #17, *High Mountain*. They're no place for a weary traveler.

Don't Give Your Wife Golf Advice

About a year after I took up golf, my wife became interested too. At first, she was happy just to ride in the cart, reading a book and enjoying the fresh air. But one day, I asked if she wanted to take a shot. She stepped up to a 125-yard par three, took a smooth swing, and knocked the ball solidly onto the green. That was it—she was hooked.

We started taking lessons together, and I quickly learned one of the most important truths in golf and marriage: don't give your wife golf advice. If your spouse wants to learn the game, let a teacher do the instructing. Encourage, support, and celebrate their progress, but don't try to be their coach. The same holds true for wives whose husbands take an interest in the game. If you want to enjoy golf together, the best thing you can do is uplift one another, not critique each other's swing.

Now, that doesn't mean you can never offer advice—but only if you're asked. And even then, keep it simple. Maybe a slightly stronger grip, a small adjustment in ball position, or a better shoulder turn. But remember this: you can't rebuild someone's golf swing while playing on the course. A single, helpful suggestion is fine, but a full lesson? That's best left for the range with a teacher.

Ephesians 5:21 reminds us to *"submit to one another out of reverence for Christ."* True partnership means serving each other's needs, not taking control. In golf and in life, encouragement goes a lot further than correction. So whether it's your spouse, a friend, or a new golfer at your club—support, celebrate, and encourage. And when advice is wanted, keep it simple.

⛳

Show Up, Keep Up, Shut Up

I once had the chance to caddy for a young man from our church—a Division I golfer fresh out of college, playing in a U.S. Open qualifier right here in Orlando. Now, I love golf, but this was different. This was high-level golf, up close and personal. The kind you usually only see on TV. It was a front-row seat to a level of focus and skill that I'd never experienced before. But my job wasn't to admire the scenery. My job was to serve.

Early on, someone told me the three golden rules of caddying: *Show up, keep up, and shut up.* That about summed it up. Be there when needed, stay engaged, and don't say a word unless asked. Simple enough, but as the round went on, I realized there was a lot of wisdom packed into those words—wisdom that stretched far beyond golf.

Jesus once said, "*Whoever wants to be great among you must be your servant"* (Mark 10:43). The world tells us to get ahead, be seen, and make a name for ourselves. But in God's kingdom, the greatest ones aren't the loudest or the most celebrated—they're the ones willing to walk alongside, ready to serve.

A good caddy doesn't make the round about himself. He cleans the clubs, studies the course, and stays ready to help. He doesn't rush ahead or lag behind. He walks step for step with the golfer, doing his job without demanding attention. That's not a bad picture of what it means to be a faithful follower of Christ. We prepare our hearts, pay attention to the needs of those around us, and stay in step with what God is doing—whether anyone notices or not.

Not many people remember who caddied for a U.S. Open qualifier. But the golfer does. And in the same way, God sees every quiet act of faithfulness. The greatest in His kingdom aren't the ones chasing recognition, but the ones humbly carrying the load for others.

Playing In God's Stadium

My wife and I recently had the chance to tee it up at a mountain-style course in North Carolina. The crisp air, the towering pines, and the drastic elevation changes made for an exhilarating round. There's something about standing on a high tee box, looking down at a fairway framed by the mountains, that makes you feel small in the best kind of way. Golf is already a humbling game, but out there, surrounded by that kind of beauty, you can't help but be in awe.

The highlight of the round, however, didn't come from a well-struck shot. On the 18th hole, after both of us had found the fairway, a young fox pup emerged from the woods and trotted right up to our golf balls. He sniffed them, pawed at them, and then—without a care in the world—started playing with them like they were his personal toys. We just stood there and laughed. There was no getting mad about it. How could you? It was a reminder that the course doesn't belong to us. We're just visitors.

Golf isn't played in a gym or a stadium. It's played in *God's stadium*. And if you don't take the time to notice the mountains, the trees, the wildlife—or even a mischievous little fox—you're missing something far greater than a good score.

"*The heavens declare the glory of God; the skies proclaim the work of his hands.*" — Psalm 19:1

WHATEVER IS NOBLE

A WHILE BACK, I WAS PLAYING A ROUND with a buddy who was having a rough day. Every shot was met with a sigh, a complaint, or a muttered, "Of course." Bad lie? Bad luck. Missed putt? Unfair greens. By the turn, his frustration was so thick you could slice it with a lob wedge. Meanwhile, I wasn't playing much better, but I had decided before the round that I was going to enjoy the day no matter what.

On the 12th hole, I hit a tee shot that rattled around in the trees like a pinball before somehow kicking out to the fairway. My buddy groaned, "Must be nice." I just laughed and said, "Hey, you've got to look for the good breaks—you'll always find the bad ones."

That's when I thought about Philippians 4:8. Paul writes, *"Whatever is true, whatever is noble, whatever is right, whatever is pure, whatever is lovely, whatever is admirable—if anything is excellent or praiseworthy—think about such things."* That's not just good life advice—it's a great golf strategy. If you focus on everything that goes wrong, that's all you'll see. But if you train your mind to find something praiseworthy—like a fortunate bounce, a friend's solid drive, or even just a beautiful day on the course—you'll start to enjoy the game a whole lot more.

The truth is, negativity doesn't just ruin your mood; it ruins your game. A bad attitude leads to bad decisions, and before you know it, your scorecard and your spirit are both taking a beating. But choosing to focus on what's good? That'll make you a better golfer and a better person to play with.

So next time you hit a bad shot, shake it off and find something good to focus on. It won't always lower your score, but it will definitely make the round more enjoyable —for you and everyone else.

A Good Name

In 2010, I entered my daughter into a contest to attend the Arnold Palmer Invitational. I didn't think much of it at the time—just one of those things you do and forget about. But a couple of months later, I got a phone call that took me completely by surprise: she had won.

The prize was more than we could have imagined. We were invited to sit in the luxury box during the tournament, my daughter got a putting lesson from Brad Faxon, and— most incredibly—we had the chance to meet Arnold Palmer himself.

That day, my wife, my daughter, and I sat down in Mr.

Palmer's office for five minutes. Now, five minutes might not seem like much, but here's what stood out: he gave us his full attention. He wasn't rushed. He wasn't distracted. He looked my daughter in the eye and encouraged her—not just in golf, but in school and in life.

Arnold Palmer's greatness wasn't just about how he played golf. It was about how he treated people. He could have been distant or disengaged, just another celebrity going through the motions. Instead, he was genuinely present, making a moment with a young girl and her family feel important.

Proverbs 22:1 says, *"A good name is to be chosen rather than great riches, and favor is better than silver or gold."* Arnold Palmer had both—riches and fame—but what made him truly great was his character. He lived in a way that prioritized people over trophies, kindness over status, and generosity over self-interest.

It's a lesson for all of us. Success is temporary, but the way we treat others leaves a lasting legacy. Whether in golf, at work, or in our daily lives, we should strive for more than achievement. We should strive for a good name.

LIFE ON THE FAIRWAY

My Daughter Sofie & Arnold Palmer
March 2011

Jim Furyk's 58:
Perfection One Shot at a Time

Jim Furyk isn't the longest hitter. He doesn't have the prettiest swing. But on August 7, 2016, he did something no one else had ever done—he shot a 58 in a PGA Tour event.

A 58. Think about that. Fourteen birdies, one bogey, and just 24 putts. It was the lowest round in PGA Tour history. But here's the thing—he didn't step onto the first tee thinking about a 58. He just hit the first shot. Then the next one. Then the next.

Golf doesn't let you skip ahead. You can't shoot 58 on the first hole. You can't win a tournament on Thursday. You play one shot at a time, one hole at a time, trusting that if you do the right things in the moment, the score will take care of itself.

Life is the same way. Lamentations 3:22-23 reminds us, *"His mercies never come to an end; they are new every morning."* God doesn't ask us to live our entire life at once. He gives us today—this shot, this hole, this moment. And if we're faithful with that, everything else falls into place.

Jim Furyk didn't set out to break a record. He just kept playing the next shot. And in the end, he made history.

So whatever you're facing today, don't get ahead of yourself. Play this shot well. Walk with God in this moment.

And trust that if you do that, the final score will be better than you ever imagined.

WATCH YOUR WORDS

THERE ARE A FEW GREAT SOUNDS ON A GOLF COURSE. The crisp *click* of a well-struck iron. The soft rattle of a birdie putt dropping into the cup. The quiet hum of nature—the rustling of trees, the distant chirp of a bird. But there's one sound I can't stand to hear out there: negative self-talk.

Now, don't get me wrong—if you're playing with your buddies, a little friendly ribbing is all part of the game. But talking down to *yourself*? That makes my skin crawl. I've heard it too many times: *I stink at this game. I'll never get better. I always mess up.* It reminds me of something much bigger than golf.

That voice of discouragement doesn't just show up on the course—it's the same voice the enemy whispers in our ears in life. *You're not good enough. You'll never improve. You're a failure.* But that's not the voice of truth. Sure, golf is hard. You're going to make mistakes. But if you want to improve, you have to give yourself a little grace. Learn from the bad shots, but don't let them define you.

Paul said it well in Ephesians 4:29: *"Do not let any*

unwholesome talk come out of your mouths, but only what is helpful for building others up." If we're called to encourage others, how much more important is it to speak life into ourselves?

So next time you catch yourself tearing yourself down on the course, take a step back. Give yourself the same patience and encouragement you'd give a friend. After all, the way you talk to yourself matters—not just in golf, but in life.

⛳

Play It Forward

Go to any golf course, and you'll see several sets of tee boxes. The farthest back are called *the tips,* then you might have *championship* or *professional* tees, followed by *men's tees,* then *ladies' tees,* and finally *senior* or *junior* tees. The problem? For the average golfer, even the so-called *men's tees* are too far back.

And if you know anything about men, you know they aren't about to play from a tee box labeled anything other than *men's.* Their pride won't allow it. So they step up, take their best swing, send the ball about 215 yards (believe it or not, the average drive for an amateur male golfer), and leave themselves a long iron or hybrid into the green. The game wasn't designed to be played that way.

That's why some courses have started renaming the tees—because the truth is, you'll play better and enjoy the game more if you play from the right tees for your skill level. Golf was never about proving how far you can hit it; it's about playing smart and having fun.

The Bible says, *"Pride comes before the fall"* (Proverbs 16:18), and nowhere is that clearer than on the golf course. A high-handicap golfer (20+) has no business playing from the back tees. If your game isn't where you'd like it to be, swallow your pride and play it forward—consider a course distance under 6,000 yards. You'll hit more greens, sink more putts, and walk off 18 with a lot less frustration.

Life's a lot like that, too. Pride can make us take on things we aren't ready for, struggle longer than we need to, and rob us of the joy that comes from playing within our God-given abilities. So in golf—and in life—don't be afraid to take a step forward. You'll enjoy the journey a whole lot more.

CHAPTER VII

Trouble Shots

"If you are going to throw a club, it is important to throw it ahead of you, down the fairway, so you don't have to waste energy going back to pick it up."
- Tommy Bolt

The Greatest Mulligan

In my weekly golf league, we have added a simple rule—everyone gets one mulligan per round. Just one.

At first, the guys weren't too sure about it. "That's not real golf," they said. "You've got to play it as it lies." But after a few rounds, they started to appreciate the idea. A single opportunity to undo a bad shot, to correct a terrible mistake, to wipe the slate clean—it changed the way we played.

One mulligan won't fix an entire round, but it can sure save you from disaster.

Life is a lot like that. We all make mistakes—bad choices, wrong turns, words we wish we could take back. And yet, many people resist the idea of grace. They think they can do it on their own, that if they just live a good enough life, everything will work out in the end. But the truth is, none of us is good enough. That's why Jesus came—to offer us the greatest mulligan of all time.

His death and resurrection didn't just give us a second chance; they gave us eternal life. And here's the best part—once you make Him Lord of your life, you're not limited to just one do-over. His mercy is endless.

1 John 1:9 says – *"If we confess our sins, he is faithful and just to forgive us our sins and to cleanse us from all unrighteousness."*

I don't know who invented the golf mulligan, but I know who invented the better one. Jesus Christ. And He's offering it to anyone who will take it.

No matter how many bad shots you've taken in life, His grace is always enough. Take the mulligan. Accept His mercy. It's the best shot you'll ever make.

Take the Drop!

There's something about standing on a par-3 tee box with water between you and the green that makes your heart beat a little faster. You take your swing, and for a moment, you're hopeful—until you hear the dreaded *splash*. Your ball is gone. Now you have a choice. Some golfers stubbornly drop another ball right where they stand, determined to "get it right." But the course designer has already given them a better option: the drop zone, often placed across the water, giving them a clear shot at the green.

Pride keeps some players from taking the drop zone. They think, *I should be able to hit this shot.* But wisdom says, *Take the better path.* The rules allow it, and it helps you recover without unnecessary struggle.

Life—and faith—work the same way. When we make mistakes, we often want to prove ourselves by trying again in our own strength. But God, in His mercy, provides a way forward. We call it grace. Instead of demanding that we fix everything on our own, He offers a fresh start—a "drop zone," if you will—so we can continue the journey with Him.

The apostle Paul reminds us, *"But he said to me, 'My grace is sufficient for you, for my power is made perfect in weakness'"* (2 Corinthians 12:9). We don't have to stand on the tee box, frustrated and stubborn. We can take the grace God provides and move forward with confidence.

⛳

The Toughest Shot In Golf

In the 2024 U.S. Open, with everything on the line, Bryson DeChambeau stepped into a bunker 55 yards from the hole and hit an incredible shot to three feet. It was the kind of moment that cements a golfer's legacy. For most amateurs, that same shot is a disaster waiting to happen. It's too far for a standard bunker shot, too short for a full iron swing, and if you haven't practiced it—which most of us haven't—your odds of success are slim.

The mid-range bunker shot is tough because it doesn't fit into a clean category. It requires feel, trust, and a willingness to make solid contact with both the ball and the sand. My best advice? Take one extra club, play the ball in the middle of your stance, lean forward, and take a controlled three-quarter swing. It won't be perfect every time, but it'll give you a fighting chance.

Life is full of these in-between moments—challenges that don't fit neatly into what we've prepared for. We pray when things fall apart, and we give thanks when blessings come, but what about the seasons in between? The times of uncertainty, waiting, or transition? If we never practice faithfulness in those moments, we're bound to struggle.

The key is to stay steady—lean into God's wisdom, trust in His provision, and take the next faithful step. Like a well-struck bunker shot, it's about contact. Not just with the sand or the ball, but with the One who steadies our hands and guides our hearts.

THE FLOP SHOT

THERE'S SOMETHING UNDENIABLY THRILLING about pulling off a perfect flop shot. The ball floats high into the

Trouble Shots

air, lands soft as a feather, and nestles next to the hole like it had GPS guidance. It's the kind of shot that makes you feel like Phil Mickelson for a moment. But let's be honest—how often does it really work out the way you planned?

For most amateur golfers, the flop shot belongs in the *no-go zone*. It's fun to practice, fun to show off, but when strokes actually matter? You're better off taking the smart play. Say you're short-sided with a bunker between you and the pin. The temptation is to try the hero shot—the full-open-face, hinge-and-hold masterpiece. But unless you're a five handicap or better, the odds are against you. Instead, play a controlled chip toward the far side of the green, give yourself a putt, and take bogey out of the equation.

There's a lesson in this for life, too. Just because you *can* do something doesn't mean you *should*. We're often drawn to flashy, high-risk moves—whether in our careers, relationships, or spiritual lives—when wisdom calls for a simpler, more reliable path. Sometimes, the best play is the one that keeps you moving forward, rather than the one that looks spectacular if it happens to work out.

So go ahead, practice your flop shots when you're out with friends. Have some fun. But when the pressure is on, play the high-percentage shot. In golf—and in life—it's not about looking impressive. It's about making wise choices that lead to the best possible outcome.

FINISHING THE ROUND

YOU'VE PROBABLY NEVER HEARD THE NAME MIKE REASOR, but in 1974, he did something no one else had done before or since. He shot the highest score ever recorded in a PGA tournament—93 over par. Now, that's not the kind of record you aim for, but there's a story behind it that's worth telling. After making the cut with two steady rounds of 72, he went horseback riding and ended up in a wreck—his horse ran straight into a tree, leaving him with a separated shoulder, torn knee ligaments, and cracked ribs. Most people would've packed it in right then and there. But not Reasor. He showed up the next day, bruised and battered, swinging a five-iron one-handed just to make it to the finish line.

His final rounds were rough—123 and 114—but he finished. And there's something to that.

I can't help but think of Paul, writing to young Timothy from a prison cell, knowing his time was short. He didn't complain about his circumstances or wish for an easier road. Instead, he said: *"For I am already being poured out as a drink offering, and the time of my departure is at hand. I have fought the good fight, I have finished the race, I have kept the faith"* (2 Timothy 4:6-7).

Reasor didn't walk away with a trophy, and Paul didn't leave behind wealth or comfort. But both of them crossed the finish line, and that's what counts. In life, we all take our share of knocks. Maybe you've had days where it feels like you're swinging one-handed, just trying to make it through. The question isn't whether the road will get tough—it will. The real question is, will you keep going? Because Paul reminds us that for those who do, "*henceforth there is laid up for me the crown of righteousness, which the Lord, the righteous judge, will award me on that day*" (2 Timothy 4:8).

So the next time life knocks you down, think of Mike Reasor. Think of Paul. And remember: no matter how the scorecard looks, finish the race. Keep swinging, even if it's one-handed. Finish the race.

CHAPTER VIII

The Game Within

"Of all the hazards, fear is the worst."
- Sam Snead

Play Smart, Not Just Bold

When I was first learning to play golf, I thought the goal was always to aim straight at the flag. That's where the hole is, so why not go right at it? But as any good golfer knows, that's not always the best strategy.

Course management is one of the most overlooked parts of the game. Most amateurs focus on their swing, their grip, or how far they can hit the ball, but they rarely think about how to *play the course*. A good player doesn't just hit shots; he thinks about where to hit them.

If you tend to miss right and there's water on the right, aim left—even if it means playing away from the pin. If out-of-bounds lurks on the tight left side of the fairway, maybe the smart play isn't the driver but a three-wood or hybrid to keep the ball in play. A shorter shot from the fairway is always better than a long shot from the penalty area.

One of my coaches used to say, *"Proper planning prevents poor performance."* He meant that a good golfer doesn't just react to bad shots—he avoids them in the first place.

The Bible says something similar: *"The prudent see danger and take refuge, but the simple keep going and pay the penalty."* (Proverbs 27:12)

A wise man recognizes where trouble lies and plays away from it. A fool charges ahead and suffers the consequences.

This principle applies to more than just golf. In life, there are plenty of places we can get into trouble—temptations, bad decisions, unhealthy relationships. The wise person isn't just the one who escapes trouble but the one who *sees it coming* and adjusts course before it's too late.

A good round of golf isn't just about how well you hit the ball. It's about how smart you play the course. The same is true in life. Play wisely.

THE GOLF SWING IN YOUR MIND

IF YOU'VE EVER TALKED WITH A GOLFER and noticed them slowly rotating their hands through the air—no club in sight—you've met someone truly in love with the game. Even when they're not golfing—they're golfing. Their mind is on their grip, their release, their tempo. Their swing is never far from their thoughts, and their body seems to instinctively rehearse the motions, as if muscle memory alone could shave strokes off their game.

That's the way prayer can be.

When Paul tells us to "pray without ceasing" (1 Thessalonians 5:17), he's not talking about spending every waking moment on our knees, eyes closed, hands folded.

He's talking about a heart posture—a way of living that keeps us connected to God throughout the day. It's a mindset of prayer, where our spirit remains in tune with Him, much like a golfer's mind stays engaged with their game, even when they're nowhere near the course.

If you can be in a golf mindset while walking through the grocery store, waiting in line at the bank, or sitting in traffic—thinking about your grip, your stance, your next round—then you can also be in a prayer mindset during those same moments. Prayer doesn't always have to be formal; it can be as natural as a golfer rehearsing their swing, an ongoing conversation with the One who is always near.

Let prayer become the rhythm of your day, the quiet motion of your thoughts, the natural response to life's challenges and joys. When you do, you'll find yourself in constant conversation with God, refining your faith as a golfer refines their swing—one motion, one moment, one prayer at a time.

The Enemy of Great Golf

Jim Collins once said, *"Good is the enemy of great."* When it comes to golf, I'd amend that a bit and say—*expectations are the enemy of great golf.*

I've lost count of how many times I've stepped onto the first tee thinking, *Today is the day. I'm going to shoot a great score, lower my handicap, maybe make a few birdies.* But the problem with expectations is they add pressure. And pressure rarely leads to good golf.

I'm not saying you shouldn't have expectations. But they need to leave room for failure—because golf isn't a game of perfection. Ben Hogan put it best: *"The guy who misses best is going to win."* Even the best players in the world don't hit every shot perfectly.

Unrealistic expectations don't just hurt your golf game—they hurt your relationships, too. We expect people to always treat us well, to never let us down. And when they do, we get frustrated. But the truth is, everyone falls short. If we're honest, we've disappointed others just as much as they've disappointed us.

The better approach? Extend grace—to others and to yourself. The Apostle Paul said, *"Bear with each other and forgive one another if any of you has a grievance against someone. Forgive as the Lord forgave you."* (Colossians 3:13)

So next time you step onto the course, let go of the

pressure. Play the game, enjoy the round, and accept that misses are part of it. And in life, do the same—because everyone, including you, is still learning.

Don't Say Water

Some of my best memories are playing golf with my dad. He wasn't the greatest golfer, but he is the best dad and a great golf buddy. One afternoon, we stepped up to a short par-3 with a forced carry over water. My dad took one look and said, *"Oh no, look at all that water."* Then he reached into his bag, pulled out an old ball, and said, *"I just bought these new ones. Better use this in case I hit it in the water."*

I think he mentioned water three more times before he ever took the club back. You'll never guess where his ball went. Straight in the water.

Now, I'm not superstitious, but I do believe in the power of the mind. Dr. Joseph Murphy once said, "As you sow in your subconscious mind, so shall you reap in your body and environment." I can't prove it scientifically, but I've seen it play out on the golf course more times than I can count.

And I've seen it work in life, too. Our words shape our

thoughts, and our thoughts shape our actions. The Bible puts it this way: *"Do not let any unwholesome talk come out of your mouths, but only what is helpful for building others up according to their needs, that it may benefit those who listen"* (*Ephesians 4:29*). And think about it—the first person listening is you.

So be positive on the course. Speak confidence, not caution. Focus on the target, not the trouble. Because whether in golf or in life, you usually end up where your mind tells you to go.

And whatever you do, don't say water.

⛳

The Walk Between Shots

There's a short nine-hole course tucked into the middle of a sleepy neighborhood that I love to play. Locals here refer to it simply as "The Winter Park 9." It's an old course, dating back to the early 1900s, and there are no golf carts allowed. You have to walk the course—and I don't mind at all.

Walking lets you feel the slope of the fairway beneath your feet, hear the rustle of the wind through the trees, and notice the way the grass gives just slightly under your shoes. It gives you time—time to think, time to breathe, time to prepare for the next shot without hurry.

Most golfers, myself included, tend to rush from shot to shot, eager to get to the next swing, hoping to recover from a mistake or build on a good one. But when you walk, there's no rushing. You're forced to slow down. To settle yourself. To simply be in the moment. That reminds me of Psalm 46:10: *"Be still, and know that I am God."*

God rarely speaks to us in the noise and hurry of life. It's in the quiet spaces, in the walk between, that we learn to trust Him. We don't always need to rush to the next thing. Sometimes, the best thing we can do is take a deep breath, be still, and know that He is in control.

So the next time you're on the course, try walking, even if just for a few holes. And in life, remember that the journey matters. Slow down. Walk with God. Let Him speak in the stillness.

PLAY THE SHOT IN FRONT OF YOU

ONE OF THE BIGGEST MISTAKES I make on the golf course is getting ahead of myself. I'll hit a poor shot, and before the ball even lands, I'm already thinking about how I can save par. *Okay, if I can just punch this up near the green, I might be able to get up and down.* Or *If I can just keep this in play, I'll take bogey and move on.*

It's easy to do. You hit one bad shot, and suddenly, instead of focusing on the next shot, you're mentally mapping out the entire hole—or worse, the rest of the round. But the problem is, you're not playing the hole in your head. You're playing the one in front of you.

The best golfers don't think five shots ahead. They focus on the *next* shot, and they hit *that* shot as well as they can. The outcome will take care of itself.

Life is no different. We spend so much time worrying about what's coming next—how things might go, what might happen if we don't get this or that right—that we forget to handle what's in front of us. Jesus understood this. He told His disciples, *"Do not worry about tomorrow, for tomorrow will worry about itself. Each day has enough trouble of its own."* (Matthew 6:34)

It's good advice for life and for golf. Worrying about the next hole won't help you hit the shot you have right now. And worrying about next month won't help you live today well.

So when you find yourself running the numbers on how to salvage the round—or your week—stop. Take a breath. Play the shot in front of you.

Remember What Matters

We tend to forget what we should remember, and remember what we should forget. It happens to all of us. You're out there on the course, hitting the ball well enough, but one bad shot sneaks in, and suddenly, it's all you can think about. Maybe you chunked an easy wedge shot, or maybe you topped a drive so bad it looked like you were playing putt-putt. Whatever it was, it sticks in your head like a bad tune you can't shake. Funny thing, though—we don't seem to hold onto the good shots the same way. We hit one pure, right on the screws, and by the next hole, it's already fading from memory.

Fred Couples was once asked what goes through his mind before a shot. His answer? He said, *"I just think of the greatest shot I've ever hit with that club."* He doesn't dwell on the worst one. He visualizes success, not failure. Then he swings.

There's wisdom in that, not just for golf but for life. Too often, we let past mistakes weigh us down, while forgetting what Christ has done for us. Paul put it plainly in Philippians 3:13-14: *"But one thing I do: forgetting what lies behind and straining forward to what lies ahead, I press on toward the goal for the prize of the upward call of God in Christ Jesus."*

The enemy would love for you to dwell on past failures. But God calls us to move forward. So next time you step onto the tee, don't let a bad shot haunt you. Let it go. Instead, hold on to the best one, picture it, and swing with confidence. That's not just good advice for golf—it's a great way to live too.

⛳

Dance with the One Who Brung Ya

One Sunday afternoon, I found myself paired with an older gentleman for a round of golf. To put it kindly, I didn't have my *A-game* that day. You've been there, I'm sure—scraping the ball around, trying to recover from bad shots, doing everything you can just to piece together something respectable.

At one point, after another less-than-stellar shot, he looked over at me and said, *"You gotta dance with the one who brung ya."* That phrase stuck with me. What he meant was simple: You can't play with the swing you *wish* you had—you have to play with the one you *actually* have that day.

The great Walter Hagen once said, *"You don't have the game you played last year or last week. You only have today's game. It may be far from your best, but that's all you've got. Harden your heart and make the best of it."*

It doesn't help to wish you had last week's game, or the game you had a few years ago. The only game at your disposal is the one you brought to the course today. And if things aren't going well, you're better off accepting it, finding a few shots you *know* you can hit, and playing within yourself until your confidence returns.

Life works the same way. Some days, you feel strong, capable, and confident. Other days, you're scrambling, doing your best just to get through. Wishing you were someone else—stronger, smarter, more put-together—doesn't help. Instead, trust the gifts and abilities God has given you for *this* moment.

As Paul reminds us in 2 Corinthians 12:9, *"My grace is sufficient for you, for my power is made perfect in weakness."* Even on your worst days—whether on the course or in life—God's grace is enough. So take a deep breath, play the game you've got, and dance with the one who brung ya.

Banana Pancakes

My wife and I have a little phrase we use when we golf: *"Just think of banana pancakes."* Banana pancakes have absolutely nothing to do with golf. And that's the whole point.

It's easy to let your mind get tangled up in swing thoughts —*Am I taking it back too fast? Am I getting too inside? Am I rotating my hips?*—until you're so locked up that you can't swing freely. Dr. Bob Rotella, the famed golf psychologist, calls it playing *unconscious*. He wrote, *"To go unconscious, to play instinctively and intuitively, you must trust your swing, you must believe that it will work"* The best golfers aren't thinking about mechanics over the ball. They've done the work on the range. Now, they just trust it.

For me, the best way to play *unconscious* is to think about something that has absolutely nothing to do with golf. And that's why we chose banana pancakes. It's silly, but it resets the mind. No tension, no overthinking, just swinging the club.

Isaiah 26:3 says, *"You keep him in perfect peace whose mind is stayed on you, because he trusts in you."* The same principle applies beyond the course. Life gives us plenty of reasons to overthink—decisions, worries, endless what-ifs. But peace comes not from analyzing everything to death, but from *trusting* the One who already has it all figured out.

So the next time you find yourself overcomplicating things—on the course or in life—try thinking of banana pancakes. Or better yet, fix your mind on the Lord. Then, take a deep breath… and let it go.

The Most Important Shot

Ben Hogan once said, *"The most important shot is the one right in front of you."* That's good advice for any golfer, but especially for us amateurs. It's easy to get ahead of ourselves—thinking about the next shot before we've even taken this one, or worrying about the tough holes coming up later in the round.

I know that feeling well. When I first started playing at my local course, no matter how well I was doing, I always dreaded hole number 12. It's a forced carry over water—something that, as a beginner, felt more like a punishment than a challenge. Even if I had played solidly through 10 and 11, I couldn't enjoy it, because in the back of my mind, hole 12 was lurking. The fear of what was ahead kept me from focusing on the shot in front of me.

Jesus had something to say about this, too. In Matthew 6:34, He reminds us, *"Do not worry about tomorrow, for tomorrow will worry about itself. Each day has enough trouble of its own."* Wise words. When we spend our energy worrying about what's next, we miss what's happening now.

So if Ben Hogan and Jesus both agree, that's good enough for me. Whether in golf or in life, the most important shot—the most important moment—is the one right in front of you. Take it one shot at a time.

CHAPTER IX

The 19th Hole

"Golf is about camaraderie and competition, but mostly, it's about the stories you tell long after the round is over."
—Anonymous

The 19th Hole

The Best Caddie You'll Ever Have

FOR MY 20TH ANNIVERSARY AS PASTOR at my church, the congregation did something special for my wife and me. They took up a collection and gifted us a two-day golf package at Streamsong, one of the finest resorts in Florida. This place is like Mecca for golf enthusiasts—tournament-level courses, top-notch restaurants, world-class practice facilities, and even a helipad. But the best part? When you play at Streamsong, you're required to use one of their caddies.

At first, I wasn't sure how I'd feel about having a stranger tagging along for my round. But after a couple of holes, I realized just how valuable he was. He knew every inch of the course—the best angles off the tee, the sneaky slopes on the greens, even where to land the ball to catch a favorable bounce. He read my shots like a book, recommended clubs I wouldn't have chosen, and encouraged me the whole way. With his help, I shot a great score and even made eagle on 18.

It got me thinking. A lot of folks hesitate to let someone else guide them through life. They figure Jesus will be a burden, a set of rules that take the fun out of living. But that couldn't be further from the truth. In Matthew 11:28-30, Jesus says, *"Come to me, all you who are weary and burdened, and I will give you rest. Take my yoke upon you and learn from me, for I am gentle and humble in heart, and you will find rest for your souls. For my yoke is easy and my burden is light."*

Jesus is the best caddie you could ever have. He designed the course—so to speak—and He knows all the ins and outs of the universe and the world you live in. Like a heavenly caddie, He knows where the sand traps are, where the fairways open up, and how to help you recover when you land in the deep rough. Life's a whole lot easier when you've got the right guide.

THE LITTLE THINGS
THAT MAKE GOLF CIVILIZED

I'VE BEEN PLAYING GOLF FOR NEARLY TWENTY YEARS NOW, and one of the things that saddens me most is seeing golf etiquette fade away. It was always part of what made the game so special to me.

I'm not talking about collared shirts and dress codes—though there's nothing wrong with looking sharp on the course. I mean the small courtesies that show respect for the game and the people playing it. Keeping pace, staying quiet while others swing, not walking in someone's putting line, letting faster players through. These are the little things that make golf feel, well, civilized.

And the funny thing is, none of this is in the rulebook. There's no penalty stroke for poor etiquette. But over the years, these customs took root because they make the game more enjoyable for everyone. Golf etiquette is really about how you interact with fellow golfers—it reflects a heart of humility and respect. Philippians 2:3-4 reminds us, *"Do nothing from selfish ambition or conceit, but in humility count others more significant than yourselves. Let each of you look not only to his own interests but also to the interests of others."* When we put others first, even in small ways, we make the game better for everyone.

That's why, when I'm helping someone new to golf, I always make sure to pass along these traditions. Park your cart on the exit side of the green so you don't slow down play. Keep up with the group in front of you—not just the one behind you. And if you're playing slower, wave the next group through.

These little things may not change your score, but they make the game better for everyone. And that, to me, is worth more than a few strokes off your handicap.

A Cloud of Witnesses

I HAVE A GOOD FRIEND THAT I'VE BEEN GOLFING WITH for about five years. He's a good golfer for sure. But...when he has to play in front of a group of people—whether that's on the first tee with groups waiting behind or the group that's waved us through—he folds like a rickety ironing board. I've done it too.

One of the most nerve-wracking moments for any golfer is stepping up to the first tee with an audience. It's one thing to hit a few practice shots on the range, but when you stand there with two or three groups waiting behind you, watching your every move, it's a different story.

Your hands tighten on the club. Your heart races. And suddenly, the only thing you can think about is not messing up. That's the quickest way to mess up.

A hesitant swing—one made with fear instead of confidence—almost never produces a good shot. The better approach? Step up, take a deep breath, and swing with purpose. You may not always hit the perfect shot, but a confident swing will serve you better than a timid one.

Hebrews 12:1 says, *"Therefore, since we are surrounded by such a great cloud of witnesses, let us throw off everything that hinders and the sin that so easily entangles. And let us run with perseverance the race marked out for us."*

While that passage refers to the faithful who have gone

before us, in golf, we experience our own version of this. The people waiting behind you, your playing partners—they're all watching. But they aren't watching to intimidate or discourage you. Instead, they serve as motivation to rise to the occasion, to step into the moment with confidence rather than fear.

The Christian life isn't much different. We don't walk this journey alone; people are always watching—some to see us stumble, others to see us succeed. Either way, our job is the same: step up, trust what we've been taught, and take the next swing with confidence.

Letting Others Play Through

Just last week, I was playing golf with one of my friends. He's a new player, still learning the game, and tends to hit the ball into trouble now and then. That means our round was a little slower than usual. Before long, I noticed the group behind us waiting on every shot. Without hesitation, I waved them through. It's just good golf etiquette—if a group behind you is playing faster, you let them go ahead. Some golfers hesitate to do this, thinking it somehow diminishes their own game, but the truth is, it makes for a better round for everyone.

The same is true in life. Too often, we see others excelling around us and feel threatened, as if their success somehow takes away from our own. But that's not how it works. Celebrating others' achievements doesn't mean you've failed—it just means they're in a season of growth and accomplishment. Your time will come, too. The Bible reminds us of this principle in *Romans 12:15*, where Paul writes, *"Rejoice with those who rejoice."* When we learn to genuinely celebrate others, we'll find that we enjoy our own journey even more.

So the next time someone in your life is thriving, don't see it as a setback for yourself. Applaud them. Encourage them. And who knows? One day, they just might return the favor when it's your turn to shine.

⛳

The Golden Rule of Golf

I DON'T BELIEVE IN KARMA—the idea that if you put good things into the universe, they'll find their way back to you. But I do believe in respecting the golf course, and more often than not when you do, it'll respect you right back.

The 19th Hole

It's not magic—it's just a good way to play.

When I take a divot in the fairway, I fill it with sand. If I see another one nearby that someone else forgot, I fill that too. When I'm in a bunker, I take a few seconds to rake it smooth, because I know how frustrating it is to land in someone else's footprint. And if I hit the green in regulation, I fix my ball mark—and maybe another one while I'm at it.

None of these things take much effort. But they make the game better for everyone.

I once played a round with an older gentleman who quietly fixed every ball mark he saw, even if he wasn't the one who made it. As we walked off the 18th green, he turned to me and said, *"You always leave the course better than you found it."* That stuck with me. It's the kind of attitude that makes golf—like life—a little smoother for the next person.

Jesus put it this way in Matthew 7:12: *"So in everything, do to others what you would have them do to you."*

That's the Golden Rule. It works in life, and it works on the golf course. Take care of the course, take care of each other, and the game will take care of you.

Ryder Cup

WITH THE EXCEPTION OF THE MASTERS, there's no greater tournament experience than the Ryder Cup. Now, I've never been to one, but every two years, watching it unfold is one of the highlights of my golf calendar. If you've never seen it, the Ryder Cup is unlike any other event in golf. It's the best players in America against the best from Europe, but here's the catch—it's not just an individual competition. It's team golf.

The game itself doesn't change, but the format does. There's alternate shot, four-ball, and, of course, the classic one-on-one matches. What makes it special is watching players rely on each other. If one golfer hits a poor shot, his teammate steps up to recover. And when it's time for those singles matches, the rest of the team is there, walking the fairways, cheering, encouraging, and rallying around their guy.

That's the way Christianity is supposed to be. Golf, by nature, is an individual game, and sometimes we treat life that way, too—like it's just us, trying to make it through on our own. But Scripture reminds us otherwise:

"And let us consider how to stir up one another to love and good works, not neglecting to meet together, as is the habit of some, but encouraging one another, and all the more as you see the Day drawing near." – Hebrews 10:24-25

We weren't meant to walk this course alone. Think of your Christian life like the Ryder Cup. Your brothers and sisters in Christ are on your team. When one of them is struggling —maybe they've hit a bad shot in life—it's your turn to step in, support them, and help them recover. And when you're the one in the rough, you'll need them to do the same for you.

We win together. We fight for each other. And all along the way, we cheer each other on.

A Champion's Character

In 2009, I had the opportunity to volunteer at PGA Tour Q-School, which was being played at Orange County National near Orlando, FL. If you're not familiar, Q-School—short for Qualifying School—was the grueling tournament that aspiring professional golfers had to survive to earn a spot on the PGA Tour. It was golf's ultimate pressure cooker, where careers were made or lost with every shot.

As a volunteer, I did a little bit of everything—shuffling players around in carts, working as a marker, and handling various odd jobs. But the most memorable moment came when I carried the standard (the scoreboard sign that displays players' scores) for a group playing 36 holes in a single day.

One of the players in that group was a young, recent University of Florida graduate named Billy. Unlike many others caught in the intense, make-or-break atmosphere of Q-School, Billy stood out. He wasn't just playing golf—he was uplifting those around him. He took time to thank volunteers and acknowledge spectators, something that many players, understandably, didn't have the mental space for in such a high-stakes event.

After four straight hours of carrying the standard, I was exhausted—and starving. Apparently, it showed, because Billy noticed. He asked if I was hungry. I admitted that I was, not really expecting anything from the conversation. Then, without hesitation, Billy jogged over to the starter's tent and grabbed me a banana and a granola bar. Here I was, volunteering at an event where he was fighting for his future, and yet he was the one looking out for me.

That young man turned out to be Billy Horschel—now an 8-time PGA Tour winner and the 2014 FedEx Cup champion. Looking back, his success isn't surprising. Long before he became a champion, he carried himself like one. Some people wait until they've made it to act the part, but Billy was already a class act when barely anyone knew his name.

THE 19TH HOLE

BETTER TOGETHER

SOME OF THE MOST ENJOYABLE ROUNDS OF GOLF I've ever played were a single-team scrambles with my friends. Now, if you're not familiar with a scramble, here's how it works: each player on a team hits a shot, and then the group picks the best one. Everyone plays their next shot from that spot, and the process repeats until the ball is holed. It's a great format because it allows players of all skill levels to contribute and makes the game more fun and forgiving.

Usually, a scramble is played in competition—teams of four battling it out to see who can go the lowest. But in a single-team scramble, there's no opponent. No leaderboard. Just you and your friends seeing how good you can be *together*.

None of us can shoot under par on our own. I certainly can't. But when we take the best shot from each of us, suddenly, we're stringing together birdies. A round that would normally be a grind turns into something special. What's tough alone becomes easier when we work together.

It reminds me of Ecclesiastes 4:9: "Two are better than one, because they have a good return for their labor." Life, like golf, isn't meant to be played alone. The Christian walk is hard enough without trying to do it all by yourself. We need people to pick us up when we're struggling, to celebrate with us when we succeed, and to remind us of the bigger picture when we get lost in the weeds.

If you've never played a single-team scramble, try it. You might just find that the best part of the game isn't how well you play—it's who you play with.

⛳

A Kingdom Perspective on Rivalry

In golf, as in life, rivalry can be a tricky thing. It can bring out the best in us—sharpening our focus, pushing us to improve, deepening our respect for others. But if we're not careful, it can also bring out the worst—pride, division, and the kind of competitive streak that makes us forget why we're even playing in the first place.

Between 2009 and 2011, the church I pastor played a yearly Ryder Cup-style match against another local church. We called it the *Congregational Cup*. Every year, for two weekends, twelve of our best golfers faced off against twelve of theirs in four-ball, alternate shot, and singles matches. And yes, we had a trophy. It sat proudly on the shelf in my office—until the year we lost, and we had to march it right over to their building and hand it off.

But you know what? I don't really remember who won which years. What I do remember is the way the matches brought us together. I remember the handshakes after a well-fought round. I remember standing around the grill at the post-tournament barbecue, laughing with guys I might not have ever met if it weren't for a little white ball and a game built on honor. I remember how two churches—different in name, different in address—proved that we weren't really on different teams at all.

The world is always trying to divide people, and sometimes, if we're not careful, the church can do the same. We get caught up comparing ministries, judging worship styles, even acting like we're competing for the same prize. But Jesus never called us to outdo one another. He called us to unity. That's why Paul urged the church in Corinth:

"I appeal to you, brothers and sisters, in the name of our Lord Jesus Christ, that all of you agree with one another in what you say and that there be no divisions among you, but that you be perfectly united in mind and thought." — 1 Corinthians 1:10

That's what made the *Congregational Cup* so special. We played against one another, sure—but we were never really opponents. We were just a bunch of men and women trying to hit a little ball straight, sometimes succeeding, sometimes failing, but always remembering that in the grand scheme of things, we were on the same side. And at the end of the day, that's the only victory that really matters.

BONUS CHAPTER

Pre-Round Devotionals

"The reason why I play golf is I'm trying to glorify God and all that He's done in my life. So for me, my identity isn't a golf score... All I'm trying to do is glorify God, and that's why I'm here."

— Scottie Scheffler, after winning The Masters in 2022.

AFTER FINISHING THIS BOOK, something didn't feel quite complete. I had shared stories, reflections, and spiritual truths drawn from a game I love—but I wanted to offer something more. Something practical. Something that could go with you—straight to the course.

That's when my wife offered a simple suggestion. "Why not include a few devotionals that golfers can read before they play?" As usual, she was right. And just like that, this final section was born.

What follows are several short pre-round devotionals—each designed to help center your heart and mind on Christ before you tee it up. Whether you're playing in a tournament, heading out with friends, or just getting a few solo holes in after work, these reflections are here to help you bring your faith onto the fairway.

My suggestion? Read one the night before your round, or even better, while you're still sipping coffee, before pulling your shoes on in the parking lot. Let God's Word be part of your warm-up routine—right alongside your stretching, swing thoughts, and putting strokes.

1 Corinthians 10:31 says, *"Whatever you do, in word or deed, do all to the glory of God."*
Golf included.

It's my prayer that these devotionals will elevate your round—not in score, necessarily, but in purpose. That they'll remind you the game can be more than competition or recreation—it can be a spiritual pursuit. A test of character. A lesson in self-control. A source of joy. And yes, even an act of worship.

So open your heart. Step onto that first tee. And play to the glory of God—Hit 'em solid today!

DEVOTIONAL #1—PERFECT PEACE
"YOU WILL KEEP HIM IN PERFECT PEACE WHOSE MIND IS STAYED ON YOU, BECAUSE HE TRUSTS IN YOU." — ISAIAH 26:3

WHEN ISAIAH wrote this prophecy to the nation of Judah, they were in deep trouble. Foreign invaders threatened them from every side. The economy was crumbling. Political chaos was everywhere. The people were anxious, fearful, and unsure of what would come next. Into all of that, Isaiah gave a simple, clear instruction: Keep your mind on God. Don't get lost in the mess—trust the One who would one day send a Savior to bring true and lasting peace.

Today, your round of golf may not feel like ancient Judah—but distractions still come from every direction. Maybe it's swing thoughts, score pressure, or a rough morning that's carried over to the course. Perhaps it's the inner pressure to perform, impress, or prove something. Let Isaiah's words guide you: center your mind on God. Fix your thoughts on Him before you grip the club and take your stance.

That might look like noticing the beauty around you—the shape of the fairway, the quiet of the trees, the feel of the breeze on your face. It might mean celebrating small wins: a well-struck shot, a moment of laughter with a friend, or just the simple joy of not being at your desk. Let each hole remind you that peace doesn't come from perfect play—but from a mind stayed on Him.

Pre-Round Prayer:

Lord, help me to keep my mind on You today—through the ups and downs, the good shots and the bad. Keep me in Your peace.

Takeaway:

Peace comes from focus on God, not your golf score.

Swing Thought:

What's one spiritual thought you want to carry with you through today's round?

_____

_____

_____

_____

_____

_____

_____

_____

_____

Devotional #2—Joy in the Journey

"Rejoice in the Lord always. I will say it again: Rejoice!"
—*Philippians 4:4*

THE APOSTLE PAUL wrote these words from prison. That detail alone should stop us in our tracks. He wasn't enjoying a perfect round, a sunny day, or an easy season. He was in chains—physically confined, yet spiritually free. Even in that dark place, he found something worth celebrating: Christ Himself.

For the Apostle Paul, joy wasn't circumstantial—it was anchored in the unchanging presence of God. And that's the kind of joy we need to carry with us, even to the golf course.

Before you tee off today, make a decision: *choose joy*. Not just the kind that comes from a long drive or sinking a tricky putt, but the kind that bubbles up from knowing that you are loved, seen, and known by the God who created you.

Golf, like life, is unpredictable. You'll slice it, you'll chunk it, you'll surprise yourself with brilliance—and disappoint yourself just as fast. But joy can still be your steady companion. Laugh more. Encourage your playing partners. Soak in the moment. Let the game humble you, and let it remind you that joy doesn't have to wait for everything to go right—it can show up just because God is with you.

Pre-Round Prayer:

Lord, fill my heart with joy today. Not because of how I play, but because I get to play—with You beside me.

Takeaway:

Joy is a choice—take it with you down every fairway.

Swing Thought:

What's one spiritual thought you want to carry with you through today's round?

DEVOTIONAL #3—THANKFUL ON THE TEE

"Give thanks in all circumstances; for this is the will of God in Christ Jesus for you." —1 Thessalonians 5:18

PAUL'S INSTRUCTION to the early church wasn't just to give thanks when things go right—it was to give thanks in all circumstances. That includes bogeys, double bogeys, lost balls, and that tee shot you wish you could have back. Gratitude doesn't mean pretending everything is perfect. It means recognizing that every moment—good or bad—is a gift from God, and an opportunity to grow in character and dependence on Him.

Before your first swing today, take a deep breath and give thanks. Thank God for the chance to be out here. For the physical ability to play. For the company of friends. For the crisp air, the shape of the fairways, the birdsong in the trees—or even the unpredictable wind that adds challenge to the day. Thank Him for time away from your desk, your phone, and the constant noise of life.

Gratitude has a way of changing the entire round. A grateful golfer is a joyful golfer. And more than that—a peaceful one. When you're thankful, you're less rattled by mistakes and more aware of the blessings all around you. So whatever this round holds—whether it's your best or your worst—begin with thanks. You'll walk a little lighter because of it.

Prayer:

Lord, thank You for today. Thank You for this round, for this course, and for the reminder that every good thing is from You.

Takeaway Thought:

Gratitude changes the game—even if the game doesn't change.

Swing Thought:

What's one spiritual thought you want to carry with you through today's round?

_____

_____

_____

_____

_____

_____

_____

_____

_____

_____

DEVOTIONAL #4—
THE GAME THAT HUMBLES YOU

"God opposes the proud but gives grace to the humble."
—James 4:6

HUMILITY ISN'T THINKING LESS OF YOURSELF—it's thinking of *yourself less*. That's not just good theology—it's great advice for your golf game, too.

Golf has a way of keeping us honest. You can feel on top of the world after a great hole, then immediately come undone with a bad bounce or a missed putt. It's a game that refuses to let you fake it for long. And that's part of what makes it so valuable—it's always offering a quiet invitation to grow in humility.

Humility on the course looks like owning your mistakes, encouraging others, and letting go of ego-driven expectations. It means not throwing clubs, making excuses, or measuring your worth by the number on your scorecard. It means remembering that golf is a gift—and you're not entitled to a perfect round.

Before you tee off today, ask God for the grace to stay low—in your posture, your attitude, and your spirit. Stay teachable. Stay grateful. And remember: God doesn't demand perfection, but He delights in a heart that's humble and open.

Prayer:

Lord, keep me grounded today. Let me walk with quiet confidence—and help me play with grace, win or lose.

Takeaway Thought:

Humility frees you from chasing perfection—enjoy every swing!

Swing Thought:

What's one spiritual thought you want to carry with you through today's round?

_____

_____

_____

_____

_____

_____

_____

_____

_____

_____

_____

_____

Devotional #5—The Long Game of Faith

"But the Lord was with Joseph and showed him steadfast love..." —Genesis 39:21

EARLY IN HIS LIFE, Joseph received a vision from God through two powerful dreams—he would one day rise to a position of great leadership, even ruling over his family. It was a clear and compelling glimpse of what was to come. But what followed was anything but a straight path to glory. His own brothers, consumed by jealousy, betrayed him and sold him into slavery. Just when things seemed to improve in Potiphar's house, false accusations landed him in prison. There, Joseph was overlooked, forgotten, and left waiting in the shadows.

Thirteen years passed. Thirteen years of silence, uncertainty, and delay. And yet, through it all, Joseph stayed faithful. He remained patient. He held on to what God had promised. And in God's perfect time, the vision came true—just as He had said.

Golf can feel the same way. You might have a great swing in practice but can't seem to find it when it matters. You may start a round full of hope, only to stumble early. But like Joseph, your story isn't over after the front nine. Stay patient. Trust the process. Some of your best shots may be just ahead. God's timing—and your game—can both surprise you.

Prayer:

Lord, help me trust Your timing. Teach me to wait well and stay steady, even when progress feels slow.

Takeaway Thought:

Patience trusts process—even when the payoff isn't immediate.

Swing Thought:

What's one spiritual thought you want to carry with you through today's round?

_____

_____

_____

_____

_____

_____

_____

_____

_____

_____

_____

_____

DEVOTIONAL #6—
WALKING THE FAIRWAY TOGETHER

"A friend loves at all times,
and a brother is born for adversity."

—Proverbs 17:17

DAVID WAS A YOUNG MAN ANOINTED TO BE KING, but his path was full of danger, fear, and opposition—especially from King Saul. In the middle of that chaos, God gave David a gift: a friend. Jonathan, Saul's own son, formed a deep and godly bond with David. He encouraged him, defended him, and even risked his life to protect him. Their friendship wasn't casual—it was covenantal. It was built on loyalty, trust, and a shared love for God.

Fellowship on the course might not look as dramatic, but it can still be deeply meaningful. Golf is a great place to grow godly friendships—to encourage someone after a bad shot, to share a laugh, or to listen when someone opens up. Some of the best conversations happen between swings.

Don't take your playing partners for granted. Whether it's a regular foursome or someone new you're paired with, look for ways to bless them. Ask a good question. Speak a kind word. Carry their bag—or their burdens—for a few holes. The round may end, but the connection might last far beyond the 18th green.

Prayer:

Lord, thank You for the people You place beside me. Help me be a good friend on and off the course.

Takeaway Thought:

Great golf memories fade—but godly friendships go the distance.

Swing Thought:

What's one spiritual thought you want to carry with you through today's round?

_____

_____

_____

_____

_____

_____

_____

_____

_____

GLOSSARY OF GOLF TERMS

Ace – A hole-in-one; when a golfer hits the ball directly from the tee into the hole with a single stroke.

Albatross (Double Eagle) – A score of three strokes under par on a single hole (e.g., scoring a 2 on a par 5).

Approach Shot – A shot played with the intention of landing the ball on the green, typically from the fairway.

Back Nine – The last nine holes of an 18-hole course.

Backspin – A backward rotation of the ball, usually generated by striking it with lofted clubs, causing it to stop quickly or spin back upon landing.

Ball Marker – A small, flat object (often a coin or disc) used to mark the position of a golf ball on the green while it is lifted.

Birdie – A score of one stroke under par on a hole.

Bogey – A score of one stroke over par on a hole.

Bunker – A sand trap or hazard on the course, typically located near greens or fairways.

Caddie – A person who carries a golfer's clubs and provides advice on course strategy.

Chip Shot – A short, low shot played around the green, designed to lift the ball briefly in the air before rolling towards the hole.

Clubface – The part of the clubhead that makes contact with the ball.

Dogleg – A hole that bends either left or right instead of running straight from tee to green.

Double Bogey – A score of two strokes over par on a hole.

Draw – A shot that curves gently from right to left for a right-handed golfer (left to right for a left-handed golfer).

Drive – The first shot hit from the tee box on a hole, typically with a driver.

Driver – The club with the largest head and longest shaft, designed for maximum distance off the tee.

Eagle – A score of two strokes under par on a hole.

Fade – A shot that curves gently from left to right for a right-handed golfer (right to left for a left-handed golfer).

Fairway – The closely mowed area of grass between the tee box and the green.

Fat Shot – A mishit where the club strikes the ground before the ball, resulting in a loss of distance.

Fore! – A warning shouted to alert others that a golf ball may be heading their way.

Gimme – A short putt conceded by an opponent in casual or match play, meaning the golfer does not have to hole it out.

Green – The closely mowed, smooth area where the hole and flagstick are located.

Grip – The way a golfer holds the club, or the rubber material wrapped around the top of the shaft.

Gross Score – The total number of strokes taken before applying any handicap adjustments.

Handicap – A numerical measure of a golfer's skill level, used to adjust scores for fair competition.

Hook – A shot that curves sharply from right to left for a right-handed golfer (left to right for a left-handed golfer).

Hosel – The part of the club where the shaft connects to the clubhead.

Iron – A type of golf club with a flat, angled face, used for a variety of shots from the fairway and rough.

Lie – The position of the ball on the ground; can be described as good, bad, tight, or buried.

Loft – The angle of the clubface that affects trajectory and distance. Higher lofted clubs (wedges) launch the ball higher but with less distance.

Match Play – A format of golf where players compete hole by hole, rather than counting total strokes.

Mulligan – An unofficial do-over shot, usually allowed in casual rounds but not in formal competition.

Net Score – A golfer's score after their handicap has been applied.

Out of Bounds (OB) – Areas outside the defined course boundaries where play is not allowed. A penalty stroke is incurred, and the shot must be replayed.

Over Par – A score higher than the designated par for a hole or round.

Par – The expected number of strokes an accomplished golfer should take to complete a hole.

Penalty Stroke – An additional stroke added to a player's score due to a rule infraction, such as hitting out of bounds or into a hazard.

PGA – The Professional Golfers' Association, which governs professional golf tours and tournaments.

Pin (Flagstick) – The pole placed in the hole on the green, indicating the location of the hole.

Pitch Shot – A short, high shot used to land the ball softly on the green.

Play Through – A courtesy in which a faster group is allowed to pass a slower group on the course.

Provisional Ball – A second ball played when a golfer believes their first ball may be lost or out of bounds.

Putt – A stroke made on the green using a putter to roll the ball toward the hole.

Rough – The longer grass surrounding the fairway and greens, making shots more difficult.

Sand Save – Successfully getting the ball out of a bunker and onto the green in one stroke.

Scramble – A popular golf format where teams play the best shot from each location, rather than each player playing their own ball.

Shank – A mishit where the ball strikes the hosel of the club, causing it to shoot off at an unintended angle.

Short Game – The part of golf that includes chipping, pitching, and putting—shots played closer to the green.

Slice – A shot that curves sharply from left to right for a right-handed golfer (right to left for a left-handed golfer).

Stroke Play – A format of golf where the winner is determined by the total number of strokes taken over the entire round.

Sweet Spot – The ideal part of the clubface to strike the ball for maximum efficiency and control.

Tee Box – The designated area where a hole begins, where players hit their first shot.

Thin Shot – A mishit where the club strikes the ball too high, causing it to fly lower and with less control.

Up and Down – When a player takes only two strokes to get the ball into the hole from off the green (one chip or pitch and one putt).

Wedge – A type of high-lofted club used for short approach shots, chipping, and bunker play.

ALSO BY PHIL AYRES

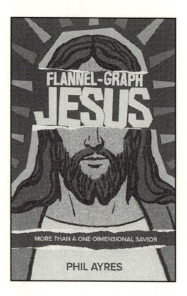

HAS YOUR MENTAL IMAGE OF JESUS been formed by storybooks, TV shows, or movies? If so, it's possible your view of Jesus may be somewhat one-dimensional.

In *"Flannel-Graph Jesus,"* Phil provides unique and captivating insights into some of the lesser known and inspiring characteristics of the Savior. For example, did you know Jesus was funny and kinda rebellious? Did you know that he had brothers and at least one sister? It's true! When you realize that Jesus is more than he seems, you'll not only fall in love with the Savior, *but you'll come to like him too.*

Available in paperback, Kindle, and Audible audiobook.

ABOUT THE AUTHOR

PHIL AYRES IS A PASTOR, teacher, and golf enthusiast who believes the game of golf teaches lessons that stretch far beyond the fairway.

As the Teaching Pastor at LifePoint Christian Church near Orlando, Florida, Phil has spent more than two decades helping people understand and connect with the Bible in meaningful ways.

Phil is also the host of *Keys for Kids* a devotional radio program for children that airs on nearly 1,000 radio stations across the United States (http://keysforkids.org).

Phil has been married to his college sweetheart, Stefanie, since 1992. Together, they've raised two grown children, AJ and Sofie, and share their home with their loyal dog, Barley.

For more from Phil, visit https://philayres.me

Email: phil@lifepointchurch.com